MY FRIENDS'

My Friends' Secrets

JOAN COLLINS

SECRETS

Conversations with my friends
about BEAUTY, HEALTH and
HAPPINESS

ANDRE DEUTSCH

contents

Photographed by John Swannell, at his London studio, 22 September 1998.

INTRODUCTION

There's a new generation of women around today.

Aged between 40 and 75, ranging from middle to late middle age, they possess more zest, vitality and creativity than many women far younger. They are a phenomenon of our era –

Generation Zest.

I CONSIDER MYSELF EXTREMELY lucky to have many female friends, most of whom have successful lives, whether as mothers, wives, actresses, writers or socialites. Each of them is uniquely different, but they are all linked by a common thread – the desire to continue to look and feel as good as possible for as long as possible. All of them are life enhancers – people with whom you wouldn't mind being wrecked on a desert island.

After *My Secrets* was published I received hundreds of letters from women around the world. Some sent me their own unique beauty tips, which made me realise the incredible diversity of people's approaches to health and beauty. But above all, women wanted to know more. So I thought why not? Why not share some of the things that my friends and I have learnt from each other?

So I began to talk to my close friends and ask them to explain what they did to enhance their looks, improve their health and get the most out of their life-style. I asked each one several specific questions, but being friends our conversation would always wander revealingly off-course.

The youngest woman I interviewed was 40, the eldest in her mid-seventies, but they all epitomise Nineties woman in one way or another. Obviously no one's personal lives or careers are ever entirely free from misfortunes or setbacks but nothing has prevented these women from leading worthwhile and fulfilled lives.

Another wonderful quality they all share is a total lack of envy or bitterness towards their 'sisters'. This lack of jealousy is the key to their glorious looks and vitality. True beauty comes from within and jealousy is its enemy. However much one tries to disguise the green-eyed monster it always reveals itself, either in a bitter expression or a look of discontent.

Far from being dissatisfied, it seems to me that many of these women are happier and more at peace with themselves now than they were in their youth. Youth may be wasted on the young but the benefits and wisdom of life experiences far outweigh any desire to be 25 again. Of the women I interviewed eight are in their forties, three in their seventies and the others, all in their fifties and sixties, are more productive than ever. Who said women were only put on this earth to produce children?

Until recently women over 40 used to be chucked on the slag heap of life, useless, used up, useful for nothing except grannyhood. They sat around in death's waiting room, bemoaning their lot, preparing for the grim reaper to beckon. But that concept has changed so unbelievably radically over the past twenty years that it seems almost laughable now.

'Who said women were only put on this earth to produce children?'

Sadly certain cultures *still* retain their innate chauvinism, which is so ingrained in religious and ethnic dogma that it may be a long time before true equality exists for them. All the women I spoke to are either American or British, from countries where the chances of living useful healthy lives into their nineties and hundreds are very real.

No one can protect themselves totally from accidents or illness, but the length of your life *can* rest largely in your hands, as does the quality of your life, the vitality you possess and the way you will look in decades to come.

Many people believe that degeneration, infirmity and illness and the decline of good looks are unavoidable after mid-life. But much of what is accepted as 'ageing' today is a result of years of disuse. Recent research indicates that *not* using your body – i.e. doing exercise of some kind – or your brain, through continuous stimulation by work, conversation and interests, is what causes people to age. Today many lives have become too sedentary – we take buses or drive instead of walking, use lifts instead of running up stairs and we don't even have to get off the sofa to change channels. Naturally the body deteriorates, the joints get stiff, the muscles atrophy. Try starting a car after it's been in the garage for a month; see how it creaks and groans.

Stretching is one of the easiest ways of using it and not losing it, yet most people don't even do *this*. It seems that in the West we are developing two distinctly different groups of people. Those whose diet consists of junk calories and fizzy drinks, and who, as they get older, spend their free time hunched over a computer or lolling in front of a TV, and those, like the women in this book, who are careful about their diet, who regularly exercise their bodies and their brains and who remain interested and therefore interesting. Which group is going to be coughing and creaking in the doctor's waiting room in years to come?

To believe that in middle age – i.e. 40 to 70 – people should put their feet up, relax and do as little as possible is *ridiculous*. Those who do will rust and rot. It's essential to keep active and, if possible, productive all through one's life-time.

It's that *gradual* premature deterioration that ruins the quality of life for so many older people, but if, like *all* the women I talked to, we take the responsibility for our health and life-style ourselves, that total deterioration can be staved off until we die of natural causes at 95 or 100.

We all know people who have become more interesting, attractive and wise over the years. Two prime examples of nonagenarians in the pink are 95-year-old Barbara Cartland (literally, too) and the 98-year-old Queen Mother. Incredibly active, productive and full of fun and interests, they have enhanced many lives.

In the next twenty years thousands of people will hit 100 – and what will their quality of life be unless they have prepared themselves for it? Our old folks' homes are full to bursting with people suffering from appalling maladies that could have been prevented.

The women I've interviewed definitely do *not* want to end up helpless and useless, and neither do I. But you can't avoid it by doing nothing. It *does* take a little effort, a bit more work and preparation and some thought. It *does* involve discipline and maintenance but then you use discipline to keep your oven clean and maintain your car, don't you?

We live in a society which worships youth despite the fact that a human lifespan is actually three score years and ten. The 'youth' we pander to is aged between 15 and 30, giving each of us only fifteen years to be the gilded ones. But there's no age limit on development. Our media has bought into the notion that youth is the only group worth cultivating, and that the rest of the population are a bunch of worthless old crocks. And as the media relentlessly seeks to seduce their demographically viable generation, the 'dumbing down' of our TV and movies be-

'Much of what is accepted as "ageing" today is a result of years of disuse.'

Photographed by Eddie Sanderson at Joan's LA apartment, 10 November 1998.

comes more pervasive. Tastelessness, vulgarity and coarseness are the order of the day on much of British and American TV and in movies today. *Nothing* is sacred and little is revered, nothing is immune from crude caricature, and authority and age are frequently sneered at.

In this atmosphere it's hard for the young to do anything but grow up arrogantly, with little respect for anything, scant discipline but always quick to demand their 'rights'. The latter meaning to be allowed to do whatever they want, to eat whatever and whenever they want, to be allowed to indulge their every whim. Exercise? Forget it. For too many it's too much effort.

Maybe this book can change a few minds –

make young people think about what their future holds when they feel as if they are no longer in their salad days and are facing another thirty, forty or fifty years of life.

I and my friends want to have maximum wellbeing and a body and mind that aren't degenerating from disuse. We want optimum health and vitality – mentally, physically, emotionally and spiritually.

I've learned a great deal from my friends. For they all have common sense and knowledge to impart and, face it, if you haven't reached the *age* of wisdom without gaining any, your life must have been a bit of a blank canvas.

JOAN COLLINS, February 1999

SHIRLEY BASSEY

THE GIRL FROM TIGER BAY

For over four decades Shirley Bassey has been one of Britain's most enduring singing stars. With more hit singles and best-selling albums than any other British female performer, her perennial appeal and popularity extend throughout the world.

She is the consummate diva-pro, larger than life, beloved and maligned – a survivor supreme, a grandmother who has no compunction about revealing her admirable cleavage even in front of the Queen.

Shirley Veronica Bassey was born on 8 January 1937 in Cardiff's docklands area, Tiger Bay. The youngest of seven children, her father was Nigerian, her mother from Yorkshire. As a child Shirley would often sing at family parties, her favourites being Al Jolson and Judy Garland. Her first job was working in a local

factory, but Shirley supplemented her wages by singing in local men's clubs.

Shirley's first break came when she was spotted by the prominent band-leader Jack Hylton who engaged her to appear in a 1955 Christmas Show at London's Adelphi Theatre.

By 1959 Shirley's unique style and phrasing had begun to emerge when she recorded 'As Long As He Needs Me' from *Oliver!* The number two single stayed in the Top 50 for thirty weeks. Ironically for someone who has since become an internationally successful recording artist, Shirley had no inkling of the extent of her talent in those early days.

By the mid-60s Shirley was at the peak of her profession, where she has remained ever since. Following in the footsteps of her idol Judy Garland, Shirley's headlining

Photographed by Leslie Bricusse at Andrew Lloyd Webber's New Year's Eve party. Cap Ferrat. 1 January 1998.

appearances at Carnegie Hall in New York became legendary. Las Vegas, Australia, Europe and the Far East were also crying out for Shirley's talents, and soon her British fans had to be content with seeing her just for a few weeks every year.

Her personal life, however, was not as successful. She married her manager Kenneth Hume in 1961 and had two children. The marriage did not last and in 1968 she married an Italian, Sergio Novak. This marriage didn't last either. Since 1979 Shirley has enjoyed the freedom of being single which 'suits me just fine' – although being linked to a number of men keeps her vibrant. For several years she's lived alone in her apartment in Monaco and the loves of her life are her family, especially her four grandsons whom she adores and sees as often as possible.

To celebrate her 60th birthday in July 1996, Shirley performed two outdoor shows in the grounds of the magnificent stately homes of Castle Howard and Althorp Park. Like her recent and extended Diamond Tour Concert in London, these spectacular extravaganzas were complete sell-outs. Her voice has lost none of its power; if anything it's now stronger, clearer, ballsier, with tremendous emotional intensity.

'I hate getting up in the morning – I'm a late person, so by the time I get the sleep out of my eyes, it's usually after two o'clock.'

I MET SHIRLEY at the Hotel du Cap in Cap d'Antibes on a cold blustery Easter Monday. Waves crashed onto the rocks outside the Eden Roc Restaurant and we drew curious glances from Susan Hampshire and her husband, lunching nearby, as we were slightly over-dressed compared to the casual holiday crowd.

Shirley wore a tight-fitting red jacket with gold buttons, and red lipstick. A rakish black fedora covered her hair, and as usual she was bubbling with personality and *joie de vivre*, her attitude and zest for life that of a woman half her age.

Thirty years ago I watched her at a recording studio, brilliantly belting out 'Goldfinger', co-written by my then husband Anthony Newley, and she's hardly changed since. The lusty laugh, the curvaceous body, the girlish walk and the bouffant coiffure – it's why she will still have her fans cheering when she's 80. We ordered Kir Royales, turbot with steamed vegetables and a bottle of Chablis, and launched straight into a fascinating breakdown of her routines, her inspirations and her priorities.

'This is almost breakfast for me,' Shirley grinned. 'I hate getting up in the morning – I'm a late person, so by the time I get the sleep out of my eyes, it's usually after two o'clock. My body clock's *appalling*, it keeps me up. I don't get to sleep until four or five and even if I'm on vacation it doesn't change. I watch films for hours – thank God for Sky TV. Then when I get up, I put hot water onto my face straight away.'

'Hot water? Isn't that unusual?'

'Yes, as hot as possible. I splash it on and I'm instantly awake. Then a hot shower or bath, then a *cold* shower, every day of my life.'

'Very good for the skin,' I commented.

'Yes. My usual breakfast is juice. I even travel with a juicer. In the morning I have fruit juice, and in the evening vegetable juice.'

'You never mix them?'

'No. You *can* mix apple with any vegetable and carrots with any fruit, but they're the only two you should combine. I can't eat meat and other protein together. It's too hard to digest and they fight. I take all the vitamins, B, D, E and C, which I get in my juice. I take the lot, multivitamins, cod liver oil, rosehip.'

'Do you cook?'

'I *love* to cook, it's the ultimate relaxation for me after coming back from an exhausting tour. I do the greatest things with left-overs. My mother was from the North of England, so they never threw anything away. She made bubble and squeak, fried from mashed potatoes and cabbage left over from Sunday dinner. I cook

Chatting with Her Majesty The Queen and Michael Caine at a reception at Windsor Castle, April 1998.

up a storm but I'm often not hungry, so sometimes I don't even eat it. Tomorrow's my fast day when I drink only juice. I have a massage and just drink lots of water and herbal tea – green tea, camomile, rosehip – I've been doing that once a week for three or four months now.'

'Do you lose weight when you fast?'

'Only water weight, but you do get rid of all the toxins. It really works because when I go on the scales – voilà! Three pounds gone.'

'You have good skin.'

'I didn't always. I used to have the most dreadful acne and the worst open pores you ever saw in your life.'

'So how did you get rid of them?' I asked.

'I think it was with age and my hormones changing. I used to have to disguise my spots by putting on one or two beauty marks, then as time went on, because my skin was so bad, I ended up with six beauty spots on stage! My skin didn't start to clear up until my late thirties. I was still painting on beauty spots and I never *heard* about cover-up stick. Then in my late thirties my skin started to change, thank God. I never wore make-up during the day, except when I had acne, but now I don't wear make-up if I'm not working, unless I'm going out.'

I looked at her closely. 'I couldn't tell if you were wearing it. It's very well blended.'

'I have it especially made for my skin by Prescriptives. It's difficult to judge the colour correctly because I make up in the bathroom with the lights on, then out in daylight it looks completely different.'

'You should always put day make-up on in a strong north light. I *always* make up in a natural light. It looks better at lunch!' I said.

Shirley shuddered. 'Oh I never do lunch, I can't. I'm still too busy getting out of bed. This is a special occasion, Joan. I don't go out much during the day. I read, watch TV, talk on the phone and then try and build up the energy either to work or to get to the gym. I usually go about seven p.m. if I'm not working. I work out for about two hours then go out to dinner. When I work out it stops me feeling down. Sometimes for no reason you have an off day. I feel terribly vulnerable on those days and all the bad things that have happened in the past come flooding back. When I'm trying to sleep at night I've found that if I've been to the gym it makes me more relaxed, so I can fight off those bad vibes and get some rest. Years ago I was trying to get a friend's wife to go and he said, "No, I don't want her to put all her sex energy into the gym."'

'Do you think that's what it is?'

'Well, I live alone and – yes – there's a lot of sexual energy released in the gym!'

'Interesting!'

We both looked out at the Mediterranean which was lashing itself into a fury and Shirley said she'd never seen it so wild before.

'When you go out during the day, you always wear a hat or a scarf and sun-glasses. Do people not recognise you?'

'I'm disguised until I open my mouth, that's always a dead giveaway,' she laughed.

'Do you do your stage make-up yourself?' I asked, as I'm always amazed by the number of actresses who can't do their own face.

'Yes, everything. Base, eyeliner, eyelashes. In fact I *over*do it, but I have to be glamorous on stage. When I first started, I just put on a little lipstick. One day the comedian's wife came backstage and gave me some advice. She said, "I was watching you right at the back of the theatre and your eyes look like tiny dots. You don't wear enough make-up. The lights drain you," she said, then she taught me how to put on the lot.'

'On my first TV show, it was wonderful to have somebody make me up, but when I saw the show it didn't look good. I didn't look like me, so I started to learn.'

'You obviously know your face, like I know mine,' I said.

'Yes, making-up is an art. I get excited about it. When I'm sitting in the dressing room, in front of my mirror, I see my face as a canvas, and I start painting it.'

'So what *don't you* eat, Shirley? You said you won't eat red meat.'

'I haven't eaten red meat for fifteen years. I eat a lot of spinach because of the iron... Vegetables, fruit, fish, chicken, but I rarely eat eggs. I'll never eat *anything* from a cow. I don't avoid meat because I'm an animal lover, I just can't digest it. I didn't find out until fifteen years ago when I had severe stomach problems and was rushed to hospital. They told me I have a narrow digestive tract and meat is very hard to digest.'

'What do you normally have for lunch?'

'Well, after I wake up I have my juice and black coffee. I wait an hour or so and then I'll have two rice cakes smothered with rose petal jam and mashed banana... because I can digest it easily.'

Moving on to another area I asked Shirley

whether she'd ever taken hormone replacement therapy.

'I used to take it and it gave me *incredible* energy.'

'So why did you stop?'

'For five years I had a pellet, which lasted for six months, but I found my energy was being drained. So I went to my gynaecologist who said, "You must take it every five months now because your body obviously needs it". I had to have a blood test every year, because of touring, for insurance. Well, it was all fine, nothing bad was showing up except my anaemia, something I was born with. Then, two years ago when I had the blood test it was shocking, it frightened me. My oestrogen level was going up and up dangerously, because of the pills. I hadn't realised because I was taking it over five years and it only showed up in my blood tests. Five years later and I asked the doctors, "What is the worst if I carry on with it?" and they said "Cancer".'

'You don't have cancer in your family though, do you?'

'No, my mother died naturally in her sleep at 80.'

'And your father?'

'He left when I was a kid. I was on the point of developing diabetes too after the HRT so I stopped it immediately.'

'What happened when you stopped taking it?' I asked.

'It took me way down. If it were a hard drug, they'd call it doing cold turkey! I became terribly anxious, but it's levelled out now. I've got the same energy, because that comes from what you eat and your life-style. I had more blood tests recently because of the tour, and everything's gone, even my anaemia.'

'It's because you're doing the right things for your body. You're eating right, you're sleeping right, you're exercising...'

'Yes and I'm not worrying anymore – well, trying not to. Getting that guilt thing off my

'Making-up is an art. I get excited about it. When I'm sitting in the dressing room, in front of my mirror, I see my face as a canvas, and I start painting it.'

back is the worst. It's a thing some women achieve with age and has nothing to do with medication. So now I just get on with it. It's *my* life, not my children's, or my grandchildren's and you've *got* to live your *own* life, you owe it to yourself. When my daughter Samantha died I was riddled with guilt, but after a time I realised I *must* get on and put the past behind me, as painful as that was.'

'You started living your own life quite young, didn't you?'

'I certainly did. At 16 I left home and went on the stage. It was quite something then because I'd led a fairly sheltered life and it was scary to go out in the world. I knew I had talent. I was given it – we're all given something and you should use it, so I used it. It's the same with tragedy – you turn it into something positive, creative. I've been through terrible times, especially when Samantha died, and you've been through them, too.'

We were both suddenly pensive. 'Why is it that nowadays so many young people expect life to be a bowl of cherries?' I asked.

'But it's *not*. It's very tough and you've got to make the best out of it!'

> *'I knew I had talent. I was given it – we're all given something and you should use it, so I used it. It's the same with tragedy – you turn it into something positive, creative.'*

We ordered coffee as the Riviera sky started to turn a nasty shade of grey and both of us gazed longingly at the dessert trolley.

I WOULD SOON HAVE to leave to catch a plane, so I asked, 'What would you take on a desert island, if you could have one beauty product?' Without a second's hesitation Shirley replied, with a grin:

'Lipstick. It's the *most* glamorous cosmetic.'

But the question as to who were her heroines provoked much more consideration.

'Cleopatra – if she was as fascinating as she's been portrayed, and my ideal man is Rhett Butler. They don't make men like that anymore'.

'They never did,' I grinned.

When the coffee arrived Shirley asked me if I'd put Canderel in it. I laughed and said yes.

'Americans do that,' said Shirley. 'They order a chocolate fudge sundae, then say... "Could I have some sweetener, please – and a Diet Coke?"'

'Have you ever seen a thin person drinking Diet Coke?' I asked. 'I never have.'

'I don't drink *any* kind of Coke, it's too full of chemicals and sugar,' said Shirley. 'I used to have a sip of brandy before going on stage, and I'd smoke too but that's all finished now. I do like to drink though – especially champagne.'

'Me too,' I said as we toasted each other with our wine.

On the bumpy plane ride back to London I thought about Shirley's passion and enthusiasm both for her work and life. At her concerts audiences have cheered her into singing many encores of 'Hey Big Spender' and several ardent fans have even sent her real diamond rings. Shirley Bassey goes from strength to strength. Head and shoulders above any of her female music contemporaries, long may she flourish.

JACQUELINE BISSET

'THE LAST OF THE GREAT ROMANTICS'

MENTION THE NAME JACKIE BISSET to most red-blooded males and they'll immediately start drooling. 'Sex,' they'll say, 'the sexiest woman ever.' One friend of mine memorably said, 'I'd do *anything* to go to bed with her. She's still devastatingly attractive.'

In 1966 I was lounging by Natalie Wood's swimming pool when Jackie, then a ravishing actress in her early twenties, came to visit. The convent-educated Scottish doctor's daughter from Reading had just arrived in Hollywood after playing a small role in the Audrey Hepburn/Albert Finney movie, *Three for the Road*. For Jackie the fame game was only just beginning. Modelling assignments had led to small parts in features: Richard Lester's *The Knack, Arrividerci Baby* and a small role in Roman Polanski's *Cul-de-Sac*.

Then in 1967 the James Bond spoof *Casino Royal* won Jackie a long-term contract at 20th Century-Fox and an impressive list of films followed. A quarter French and bi-lingual, she appeared in many foreign productions. Indeed in 1972 Francois Truffaut cast Bisset in *Day for Night*, the film which won an Oscar for Best Foreign Language Film.

'She'll go far,' commented Natalie, who should know – and indeed she did. Jackie oozed sexuality. Even as women we all sensed it immediately as we sat watching our children in Natalie's pool, and gossiped the afternoon away.

In the late 70s Jacqueline Bisset emerged as one of the international film world's most lustrous stars. She graced the covers of both *Newsweek* and *People* in the same week and produced the extremely succcessful *Rich and Famous*, acting opposite Candice Bergen.

Jackie has starred opposite a series of Hollywood's most glamorous leading men: Frank Sinatra, Dean Martin, Paul Newman, Steve McQueen, Marcello Mastroianni, Tony Curtis and Jean-Paul Belmondo. But it was with 1977's *The Deep* that she became a cult sensation. The vision of Jackie coming out of the sea in her soaking wet tight white T-shirt guaranteed the film's success, and gave her major sex-symbol status.

Twenty years on she still turns heads, the frank blue-green gaze is as faintly quizzical and ingenuous as ever and she exudes a lady-like sexuality. Jackie has never married, preferring serial monogamy with attractive men – actor Michael Sarrazin, restaurateur and producer Victor Drai, Russian ballet dancer Alexander Godunov. Currently her swain is Emin, a martial arts expert.

WE MET AT MY apartment in Los Angeles on a hot May afternoon. Jackie was wearing a casually chic black trouser suit and, like the English women we are, we took tea and biscuits at 4 o'clock.

Shy and charming with extraordinary light blue-green eyes, Jackie has a disarmingly direct gaze, which can turn into a lethal come-hither look, on or off screen. I began by asking her how she usually starts her day and she sighed and shook her head.

'I remember when I used to take my mail outside, open it and feel the sun on me, and sort of lie there, read it and then start my day. Now I can't even find five minutes to do that, which is just as well because my skin would look like an old boot.'

'Is that because you have so much more to do these days?' I asked.

'I don't know what it is – telephone calls, exercising the dog, exercising *myself*.'

'Do you have an exercise machine?'

'Well basically I have various bits of equipment, but I don't use it very well. I *must* perspire... that's important for me, because my body and face have a tendency to retain water. Last night I went to a restaurant and ate a Moroccan-style tagine. I wasn't hungry when we went but when I left I knew I'd overdone it. This morning I was absolutely unphotographable. My hands were swollen, my face was swollen and *that's* what happens when I eat relatively normal food. I was with some friends, so I didn't want to be a pain in the neck and say I just wanted a salad. I ordered dinner, *then* I remembered today's photo session. So this morning I had to take a water pill, exercise and *really* sweat. Finally my face has come down.'

'But your bone structure's still fantastic. It's hard to believe you could look that bad.'

'Now I look fine, but my housekeeper didn't believe how much better I looked this afternoon than this morning. It's salt retention – it's like an allergy so it's *crucial* that I stay away from it.'

'You know salt's in *everything* in America, even bread.'

'Yes, it's even in cakes.' She took a bite of a shortbread biscuit and smiled her dazzling smile. 'I really do love biscuits. So *no* salt and exercise are very important for me. As for skin care I don't have any magic creams that I rave about, just as long as they don't contain a lot of perfume. However, I have *just* become conscious about all the stuff you put *on* your

Photographed by Eddie Sanderson at Joan's LA apartment, 14 May 1998.

body. When you think about it, even something like a nicotine patch, *anything* you put on your skin, is absorbed into your system. I find it frightfully worrying because I put *gobs* of moisturiser on and deodorants and I've been doing so for years.'

'I've never heard that before. I've never even *thought* about that.'

'I've really become more aware of how instantaneous it is since I've come across people using nicotine or HRT patches.'

'So you don't use any products with perfume in them?' I asked.

'I've never liked perfume. I never even use those wet towels they give you on airplanes.'

'They can carry *tons* of germs,' I shuddered, 'if they haven't been sterilised properly. Another thing you should never do when you're in a public loo is to dry your hands with the hot air machine. Apparently that's *filled* with germs.'

'Of course, heat breeds germs. You should *always* wash your hands for at least twenty seconds, otherwise the soap's not rinsed away,' said Jackie. 'I wash my hands before I go into the loo as well as after, because I'm bringing in dirt from the outside. After I wash them, I *don't* touch the door handle and *don't* touch the faucet. When I turn the water off, I take the towel then use it to turn off the taps.'

'That's quite a production,' I said, then poured more tea as we ruminated on loo etiquette.

'Do you realise,' Jackie continued, 'that even if you kiss someone on the cheek, you can get their germs. Think of all the kisses you receive from strangers today.'

'I *hate* that. Where did this horrible habit of kissing perfect strangers come from? Now people you don't even know come up and kiss you on the *lips*,' I said.

Jackie laughed. 'I just move fast if I see someone heading my way with pursed lips.'

'I went to a party at somebody's house the other night whom I didn't know well. He advanced towards me then *rubbed* his sweaty face all over mine, kissing me on one cheek and then the other. My whole face was *covered* in his sweat. What should one do in that case?' I asked. 'You *can't* back away from your host. Sometimes I'll say "I've got terrible flu", but people say, "I don't care I just want to kiss you." '

Jackie added, laughing, 'If I don't know them I'm quite rude and just turn away.'

I then asked Jackie about her basic beauty routine. She explained that she's extremely careful about what she puts on her skin.

'I don't like too much water on my skin because it dries me out completely, since I have a very dry skin. I rarely have more than one shower a day and if I need to wash again I wash in bits. I seldom use soap on my face, only if I've been gardening and I'm covered with dirt.'

'When you're out do you wear moisturiser or make-up? You look as if you don't wear much make-up – it's a good natural look.'

'When my face is wet from the shower I use Aida Grey make-up and moisturiser – I've been using it for years – then I put on a light cream and dot powder on my nose and odd places.'

But most important to Jackie is her inner equilibrium. 'What's *crucial* to me, Joan, is *balance*, my feeling of *balance*. I need to have

'Look, I'm never going to look like an eighteen-year-old girl again and I honestly don't give a damn.'

both feet planted securely on the ground. Some days I'm off kilter and feel slightly unbalanced. Sure I'm disciplined, I can build up to being in control, but it takes me a long time. I do an hour on my treadmill, where I watch tapes, and answer the phone, which usually starts me back on track mentally and physically. I don't have my own gym but I have a treadmill, a rowing machine and a bicycle which saves me an hour of going out to the gym. I *don't* want to be seen slopping around in gym clothes. I don't find it boring because I need to sweat, as long as I have something to watch on television. Sometimes I start exercising at eleven o'clock at night if Emin isn't here, and I try to do it five times a week.'

'That's pretty good,' I said. 'What exercise do you do for your arms?'

'When I garden and sweep the yard I do lots of movements. If you garden you're always doing things. Sometimes I do arm curls, but I don't do my whole body... I *should* do sit-ups, stomach exercises. I have a desperate need of it but I *don't*. I hate it so much I just won't.'

'Whatever it is you're doing it's working well,' I commented.

'No, it's not working, but I *need* to do it,' she said. 'Look, I'm never going to look like an eighteen-year-old girl again and I honestly don't give a damn. I would love it if it just happened, but I'm not prepared to put in four hours straining and sweating in the day which I could make my own. I'd rather spend time reading, talking to friends and simply muddling around the house.'

'Right. What do you think of Cher? She exercises herself ferociously yet she's said she's miserable being in her fifties.'

'I think it's *sick* to spend so many hours working out,' said Jackie vehemently. 'I also have a thing about men exercising too much unless it's part of their job. I don't like the idea of a man wasting his time so frivolously. If he

was building a house or helping the world it would be different.'

'Doesn't Emin work out?' I asked.

'Emin is a martial artist and he's *extremely* fit. He doesn't want to bulk up, so he does it slowly.'

We moved on to the all-important question of diet.

'I *never* follow diets. I just eat very healthily. But I do have a weakness for bread and mayonnaise so it's hard. The food in Los Angeles has become very good. In the past that wasn't the case, so often I'd skip a meal.'

'But don't you think the portions that you're served in America are far too large?' I asked.

'That doesn't bother me because I have a voracious appetite,' said Jackie. 'For breakfast my housekeeper makes brown muffins with prunes and dates or banana, then I have cereal with some fibre. All Bran's good, with low fat milk and one big cup of coffee, fresh brewed with white sugar... I can't get into that sugarette. I believe all that stuff might be cancerous anyway.'

'I've heard that,' I said, 'but it's only been proven with rats, not humans.'

'Wait and see. I never gave up butter. I've always been convinced that margarine is an evil product. I stay away from it and I don't believe in drinking too much coffee, either. Mind you, I like barbecued food. I know it's bad for you too, but it's *so* delicious. I even think toast is probably not good for you either.'

'But you know, Jackie, even if we just ate salads and veggies, they've had pesticides sprayed all over them. We'd have to scrub them with soap to get those poisons off. And this GM food thing is a *nightmare*.'

'I know, but mainly I eat vegetables. I keep a plate full of assorted cooked vegetables in the fridge. I make a good vinaigrette with cold pressed olive oil, French mustard, vinegar and lemon and I basically just have steamed broccoli, green beans, Brussels sprouts, zucchini and sometimes carrots to snack on.'

'I love Marks and Spencer food, do you?' I asked.

'I never buy processed or prepared food, but if there was a Marks round the corner I probably would. When I'm in London I'm too busy catching up with all the English things I love, like Scotch eggs, pork pies, Ryvita and Marmite. But I try to avoid yeast things – because if your body gets unbalanced, which mine has a tendency to do, yeast is not good for you.'

'Since you're a quarter French, you probably like to have wine with your meals,' I said.

'I drink everything, wine, spirits, coffee – everything except diet drinks or fizzy sodas,' she said.

'*No* one I've talked to for this book ever has diet or fizzy drinks, which is probably one of the reasons they all look so great,' I added.

'I drink lots of water but not from the tap in America. When I'm in Scotland I drink tap water because it's from the river which makes a difference. It's crucial for me to drink lots of

water, but it's a daily battle to get everything balanced in my body. If I drink masses of water and don't eat the right things it doesn't work.'

'So how do you relax or de-stress at the end of the day or when you finish shooting?' I asked.

'I don't. I don't know how to,' she laughed.

'Then what is your basic philosophy of life? What makes Jackie Bisset tick?'

'I'd say my basic philosophy of life for my *physical* looks is: don't think bad thoughts because they show on your face. The thoughts

you think are what you become. Mean thoughts make mean faces. Oh, I occasionally allow myself a little bit of a gossip, but not often. I can get on the criticism bandwagon like everybody else, but since I'm a Virgo it's detrimental to my spirit. Plus I know that when I'm doing it I'm being evil and it doesn't suit me, because that's not my basic personality. It only usually happens on a movie set, when I'm bored. Then I want to know absolutely *everything* that's happening. My make-up man always knows everything, and has antennae like radar.'

'Make-up men *always* know,' I laughed. 'Do you remember when we first met?'

'Don Feld, the designer, brought me to a party at your house. You were married to Tony Newley and wearing a white boa and long dress but we didn't really speak. Then I saw you again at the Connaught. I was having one of the only lunches I'd ever had with my father in a smart place. We were sitting in the bar and you walked in with a big black hat and I completely lost my father. He *went* – I just lost him! That must have been twenty-five years ago.'

'I thought we first met at Natalie's house.'

'Oh yes, at a pool party. Julie Christie and Warren Beatty were there, too. In the evening you were going to The Factory disco so you had rollers in, with a scarf over them. That night I saw you at The Factory and you looked absolutely incredible...'

'Well, I had spent the whole day in rollers!' I joked. 'Anyway, if you had to take one beauty enhancer on a desert island, mental, physical or emotional – what would it be?'

'I was going to say Emin.' She smiled mischievously. I asked Jackie if she had any heroes or heroines.

'Jeanne Moreau. Because she's the most extraordinary actress and woman. As a young girl she was everything I didn't know about, both good *and* bad. Mostly for her female spirit, which was both Machiavellian and charming. She's also the subtext of femininity, as opposed to being sweet and shy and *nice*. I was totally overwhelmed by the kind of movies she did, subjects that women were *never* able to make movies about. She gambled, she played women who lived their lives the way they wanted to. Oh, she made masses of extraordinary films. *Jules et Jim, La Baie des Anges* – she even played a schoolteacher who was a pyromaniac. Jeanne was definitely my major heroine. But there are others. I thought Albert Schweitzer was an extraordinary person, in what he achieved and I love poets – people like W. H. Auden – and novelist Henry Miller – I always like old faces – old, lined faces – those are the sort of faces I like. Picasso had a wonderful gnarled face. I wasn't ever really into pretty boy faces.'

'Do you feel that you could ever say, "I've had enough, I don't want to be in love anymore, I don't want to have sex any more?" I asked. 'Do you feel that one day you won't want that anymore? Or do you always need a man to be with you?'

'I don't think of it that way,' Jackie smiled. 'I don't say, "Oh I need some sex so I must find a man." Most women don't. I think it happens when you become close to somebody and want to have a full relationship – so I can't see any reason why I would change the way I am. There's such a *difference* between a relationship with a friend and a relationship with a lover, such a different intimacy. My friends are *incredibly* important to me, but, unlike some women, I've never had affairs with them. Some people say, "Oh we're good friends, we sleep together from time to time." I never wanted that. Quite a few women *do* have casual relationships with their friends, but I've always been involved in passionate relationships.'

'You've always had someone in your life. Of all the women I know, you are most like me in that respect. A lot of women over 50 I've talked to say that they're not interested in sex anymore. They're perfectly happy being on their own, don't want a man, haven't had a man for three years, five years, ten years even.'

'It's amazing how unappealing a lot of men are out here.'

'Ah but are they being truthful?' Jackie smiled slyly.

'Well, I've not given them a lie detector test! I know that if it weren't the *right* man, I wouldn't want to have just anybody in my life – I'd much rather be alone. But there are so *few* right men for women over 40. I'm very lucky to be with Robin who is fabulous, but if he wasn't in my life I don't think I'd be looking.'

'It's amazing how unappealing a lot of men are out here. It's not that they're bad *people*. There are lots of people in LA who seem asexual; they have ambition and business drive, but not much sexuality,' said Jackie.

'Particularly with men in the movie business, so much of their energy goes into working and striving to be top of the heap, that they don't think about sex. Or they think of sex as a meal, like, "I've got to have a woman so I'll send for a hooker",' I said.

'I've heard a lot of women talking in that vein too, saying, I can't be bothered with a relationship, I don't want all the work it entails. Or else they say there are no men around. Well, that's because they're looking at the wrong group of men. There are masses of men around, and very pleasant men too. But so many actresses are spoilt, and so distorted in their view of fame and success that they won't look outside the movie industry and acknowledge that those men do exist. They think "that man can't take me where I want to go, they can't keep up with me, they're not in my league". But they're making a mistake. There *are* lots of men who could make them really happy,' Jackie said adamantly.

'*Exactly*,' I agreed, 'and you *don't* have to go for a man with the power, success and money. I've never liked that sort of man anyway, they're usually *so* bigheaded and often boring.'

'Right, and he's usually never there because he's too busy working,' said Jackie.

'You've always been with really interesting, attractive men and I admire the fact that you've never married. Have you never had insecurities about *not* being married?'

Jackie laughed. 'I have insecurities, Joan, I have *lots* of insecurities. But they're in another area. The reason I haven't married is probably *because* of certain insecurities. It's my way of trying *not* to be in the position that my mother was in. Basically, having been very unwell, she was left in a situation where she was unable to look after herself. I think that certainly coloured the way I feel. I *love* men, and I understand them very well, although many of them are rascals, but I've always tended to like the rascals to a certain degree. Emin's not a rascal but he looks a little bit like one. We've been together for two years. Although he has a slightly naughty face he's a very faithful person. He's

very playful and he's got sex appeal, he treats me with great respect and I respect him. He's my best friend, a very special person and we laugh a lot together. The most important thing for me is to be around people I can respect, who have dignity and who treat others with dignity. I *need* to be part of a forward flowing group, action, *ambience*, everything. I get stressed easily and the only way I can really keep my cool is to avoid people who are "a vexation to the spirit", as "The Desiderata" says.'

'What do you think about this saying – "There are only two kinds of people in the world, drains and radiators"?' I asked.

'I like that,' said Jackie. 'There was a period when I was surrounded by drains and I thought, I *can't* keep giving like this. So I decided to buy a radiator! A nice hot radiator. I think I'm a radiator, actually.'

I laughed. 'Me too! I hope I've never been a drain. I try not to be.' I asked Jackie about her next project.

'A film called *A Dangerous Beauty*. It's set in Venice, in 1560, and it's about a woman who teaches her daughter to be a successful courtesan, as she once was. That was one of the few options available at that time to females, other than being a wife, a nun, or a scullery maid – can you imagine?' She laughed.

'We've come a long way baby,' I said.

'But there's more to come,' said Jackie. '*Lots* more, I hope.'

It was time to pose for Eddie, and as we laughed and joked our way through the session I thought what a truly *nice*, wonderfully earthy woman she was.

Later that day I mentioned to a male friend that I'd just spent the afternoon interviewing Jackie.

'Phwoar, lucky you,' he sighed. 'I *really* fancy her. Could you get me her number?'

Jacqueline Bisset, still one of the sexiest women in the world, and one of the nicest.

ACKNOWLEDGED AS ONE of Britain's great beauties, Shakira Caine is also one of the warmest and most sympathetic of friends. When I first met her before her marriage to Michael she was extremely pretty but quite shy. Now, 26 years later, she is much more beautiful and serene, with lustrous black hair and an enviably firm jawline.

Shakira Baksh was born in British Guiana (now Guyana) in the late 1940s to Kashmiri Indian parents. Sadly her father died when she was very young so her mother, Saab, supported her family of two sons and Shakira by dressmaking – Shakira herself worked as a secretary in a government office.

Unbeknownst to Shakira, her mother entered her for the Miss Guyana beauty pageant when she was 18. Wearing a dress her mother had made, she won and, as Miss Guyana, went to London for the finals of the Miss World Contest. She came second but her exotic beauty quickly opened the doors of the modelling world and she signed with the Gavin Robinson Agency.

In 1970 Michael Caine saw the ravishing Shakira in a coffee commercial on TV. Immediately smitten, he called his agent Denis Selinger and asked him to try to fix up a date with her.

Two years later they were married and their daughter Natasha was born in 1973.

The Caines are equally at home in Los Angeles where they lived for ten years, Miami, where Michael has another of his successful restaurants, and England where they have homes in London and the country. Michael and Shakira are one of London's most popular couples, and have been extremely happily married for over twenty-five years.

Shakira and I met for lunch at Harry's Bar

SHAKIRA CAINE
SERENELY STYLISH

Photographed by Eddie Sanderson at the Athenaeum Hotel. London, 18 June 1998.

on a curious mid-summer London day in which it either pelted rain or blazed sunshine. As usual she was supremely elegant in a pale beige suit, and a beautiful pair of earrings of her own design, her jet hair casually framing her perfect oval face. Her skin is pale olive and crimson lipstick accentuated her exotic looks.

Shakira ordered simply, eschewing a starter, and we allowed ourselves one Bellini each before we got down to the business of the day.

'I think you are one of the most beautiful women in England and many people agree. You have an incredible jawline and gorgeous skin so let us into some of your beauty secrets.'

Shakira smiled. 'I just wash my face with soap and water. I don't use any creams except Retin A, which is available on prescription in the UK, once a week. I've been using it for ages, but you have to be careful because it can dry the skin and make it peel forever.'

'You have absolutely *no* wrinkles, lines, sags, *nothing*. I mean your face is flawless,' I said admiring it.

'Oh, I see flaws but I cover them up with make-up and stuff,' she laughed.

'You don't wear much make-up.' I inspected her face closely.

'No, I don't. I use the same powder I've been using for ten years and just eye make-up. I use Mac eye make-up and lipstick and that's it.'

'You don't use any base?' I asked.

'No, I don't.'

'But you wear a moisturiser?'

'I don't. I hate to tell you I don't use anything. I've been using this Lancôme powder for a long time and I've recommended it to everybody. It's dual finish, combination, like a pressed powder and foundation. I literally throw it on and that's all I do,' said Shakira.

'You make it sound too easy. You also have such beautiful shiny hair. What's the secret?'

'I swim a lot so I'm sure something is going to go drastically wrong with my hair. I have *slightly* grey hair in some places, which I colour myself but I don't look after it as much as I should. I wish I could be more disciplined.'

'You're just one of those natural beauties who doesn't *need* to do much. You're *very* lucky. You don't even put on night cream?'

'Nothing,' she laughed.

'What about exercise?' I asked.

'I swim religiously, it's an addiction of mine. I must swim every day if possible. When things get too much, when I feel I can't cope, I swim for an hour. Then I come back to my desk and cope with Michael and Natasha, my mother, whatever's in my life.'

'So you think swimming is stress-relieving?' I said.

'I think it's important to find out what *you* can do to relieve stress. Sometimes people need to go to sleep for an hour, and sometimes in the middle of the day I've got to put my feet up, take the phone off the hook and just relax. Each individual has to find their own way of coping with stress; swimming just happens to work for me.'

'It's also stress-relieving for my daughter Katy,' I said.

'Then it's important for her too. When they're young you must teach and encourage your girls to take care of themselves. They must make time for massages, for swimming, for a walk in the park, for a little time when they can be on their own because that's when you build up inner strength, *that's* when you can cope with the world. I've told Natasha that. I do have a lot of massages and I found a wonderful Japanese woman who does shiatsu massage. It's *fantastic*. She presses on a point in your back and presses *hard* until finally when she presses it no longer hurts. I also think that when you hold a lot of pent-up feelings and pent-up emotions inside you massage releases them.'

After we finished lunch we walked slowly

down Curzon Street in the hot June sunshine to a suite in the Athenaeum Hotel.

'What about diet?' I asked after we settled down and ordered tea.

'I'm careful, not *extremely* so but if I see the weight piling on, I diet.'

'I noticed you didn't have any bread at lunch,' I said.

'No, because I had risotto. If I'm having something like risotto, I don't want to eat bread. I don't particularly like meat. I eat chicken from time to time but I'm not trying to be a vegetarian. I prefer to eat fish or vegetables. And I drink wine. Not a lot, I prefer vodka. I found that wine is very acidic and it gives me aches and pains. If I drink a lot of wine I feel like death the next day. If I drink a lot of vodka I feel great the next day.'

'Really? If I drink a lot of vodka it makes me feel drunk,' I laughed.

'It can. It gets into your head really quickly.'

'Do you take vitamins?'

'I try to be consistent with vitamins. I started to take Dong quai for menopause and it's making a big difference to how I feel.'

'But you don't take HRT?'

'I used to have the implant but I stopped because I found that I was feeling bloated,' she said. 'Now I take this plant gel called Estrogel.'

We moved onto the revealing subject of heroines:

'I have so many heroines, Joan. I admire *any* woman with children who works hard, like you, or women like my mother who have to cope with their children without a father. My mother is my heroine. As you know, my father

died when I was five and she had to put us through high school... she worked to take care of us. I think to take that on is just amazing.'

'Did your brothers spoil you?' I asked.

'No, I'm the eldest in our family. I didn't grow up with a father, so I took on the role of mother at a very young age. My mother made clothes, which is where my love of clothes comes from. She made wonderful dresses and beautiful things. We lived above the shop, and she had a team of women working downstairs so I was in charge of running our house as a teenager. I remember thinking at 16 that I had to start cooking because everyone was hungry. I find it extraordinary to see women like my mother, and like you, who have raised three kids, because I know you *constantly* think and worry about them, and will continue to do so even when they are adults,' she said.

'Yes, I told Tara who's expecting her first baby, "You do realise that this is not just a ten, fifteen or twenty year occupation, you're going to be a mother *forever*", I said. I have an American girlfriend who said, "How do you cope with two children under the age of eight, no husband and a career? It's *impossible*".'

'Yes, all your energy is taken up running those kids' lives. It's always at the back of your mind, constantly in your thoughts. But you have to take control. A lot of people tell me I spoil my daughter but I think why not? What the hell. I give her anything she wants. I give it to her because I *want* to. I wish my mother had been able to spoil me. My friends tell me that Natasha's going on too many holidays, but when Michael and I die she's going to enjoy

'If I drink a lot of wine I feel like death the next day. If I drink a lot of vodka I feel great the next day.'

everything anyway, so why shouldn't she enjoy it *with* me? It's a part of my life and it's giving me pleasure. I think it's important to spoil your children.'

'Natasha's not spoiled, she's a lovely young woman,' I said.

'No, she's not spoiled but there are times when people do say you're doing too much for her – she should do this or that. But I've chosen to do that for her, so why not?'

> ## 'My own self-esteem is so much higher now than when I was in my twenties and men were trying to jump me all the time.'

'I feel the same way. Some people resent the fact that you love somebody so much that their happiness and their enjoyment comes before your own. Katy was so thrilled when I gave her a membership to a fabulous health club that it gave me pleasure too. Don't you love buying Natasha clothes?'

'I *adore* buying her clothes. I spend the whole day in shops with her and buy her tons of things. If she loves an outfit in my wardrobe she can have it. How can you explain to somebody that this child is more important than what *you* want? You could *never* explain that feeling to someone who doesn't have kids, they wouldn't understand.'

'Part of being a woman is giving un-conditional love. I'm sure that whatever happened to Natasha you'd always be there for her,' I said. 'I think that's a true measure of love – that it's unconditional. One has that with a man

to some extent, but there are things one *couldn't* forgive in a man, like brutality.'

'It's the *worst*. Women who put up with that think very little of themselves. They have low self-esteem,' she said.

'Where do you think that self-esteem comes from? Do you think you're born with it, do you think it comes from your family?'

'I think from *yourself*. You've just got to drag it out of yourself,' she said.

'How do you tell your daughters that they've got to have self-esteem? How do you give somebody self-esteem?' I asked.

'It comes from maturity and getting older. I remember being in my twenties and having very low self-esteem, then one day I grew up and said this is enough.'

'My own self-esteem is so much higher now, than when I was in my twenties and men were trying to jump me all the time. I thought then that being physically attractive was the only important thing in life,' I said.

'So what made you change? Did it happen over a period of time?' she asked.

'No, it was gradual. I certainly didn't get self-esteem from most of the men I was with. It finally came from what I achieved *myself*. The realisation dawned that I was an intelligent, smart woman who was actually a good *person* too. I've never wished anyone ill or been envious of anyone. Jealousy is so destructive. But I did find being on *Dynasty* hard because I became totally associated with the role I played. "Oh she's such a conniving bitch." I had to live with that image of a hard, cold toughie for *years*.'

'In the end, Joan, you did *Dynasty* to survive. You were a single mother, you had to support three kids, you had to pay bills... Sometimes you must say to hell with what everybody thinks, to hell with what they say about you, *you* know that you're doing it for your own reasons. Other people don't live your

life and they have no right to criticise or question what you're doing. I'm doing my jewellery because I want to, and I'm making money doing it so why not?'

I asked Shakira the history of the beautiful, self-designed, gold and pearl earrings with Swarovski crystal that she was wearing.

'I started with the idea of taking *real* Indian jewellery and making costume jewellery out of it about ten years ago,' she said.

'Are you still doing that? Those earrings look more modern,' I remarked.

'I'll do some of these, but many of the pieces that I'm selling are very ethnic. I design them myself and my inspiration comes from India and jewellery books. Sometimes an idea just sparks off another idea. I use semi-precious stones, and those pieces are sold in Harrods and Harvey Nichols for about £150. I've got a different line for the Home Shopping Network on TV in America. I'm enjoying it and it's given me a freedom and independence that I probably wouldn't have had. Suddenly I realised that I could go out and make it on my own,' she said.

'It's very important for women to find themselves as they get older,' I said.

'What gives women self-esteem is knowing that they *can* go out and do it themselves and they don't necessarily *need* a guy. Too many women we know think they can't survive unless they're with a man who can buy them a first-class ticket to New York, but it's not true.

'I think many women over a certain age – over 40, or 50 – a lot of them do feel guilty if they take time for themselves.'

They *could* do it if they got off their arses and applied themselves.'

'What's your philosophy of life?' I asked.

'To live one day at a time and make that day *fantastic*, not to worry too much about what *could* have been or what is *going* to be, but just to live the moment, enjoy *every* second, and not hurt anyone.'

'Shakira, you're incredibly stylish, and you always look wonderful, even in blue jeans and an old sweater. You've been named Best Dressed on Eleanor Lambert's List several times. What's the secret of your eternal style?'

'I was surprised to find myself on that list because I don't always buy St Laurent and Dior, although I love designer clothes. I *could* spend all my money on clothes – I adore clothes, but I buy sensibly – suits, trousers and jackets. I look for comfort in clothes, things I can wear and forget about, as opposed to worrying about how I look.'

'You've got fantastic arms but you always cover them up. Why?'

'I cover my whole body,' she laughed.

'But why cover up such beautiful arms?' I asked.

'When I'm in the sun I'll wear a bathing suit and sarong, but in our English climate you very rarely have the opportunity to show your arms. Only in evening clothes.'

'That's a great Ralph Lauren suit and white shirt you're wearing.'

'The shirt's from Gap,' she said. 'And it's also stretchy. I *love* white shirts, I have about sixty. Last night I wore a Giorgio Armani organdie white shirt. There's something quite sexy about white shirts.'

'Don't you think a lot of women of this generation are able to express themselves much better than their mothers and grandmothers?' I asked.

'Yes, it's wonderful – that's what makes us unique. Many women in our mothers' age group kept everything down. If they were ill they wouldn't express how they felt. I hate that. In those days it was almost taboo to disagree with a man. I think they didn't even know what they really liked whereas women today do. I think that's important if you're with a man. I'm with Michael and he takes over my life. He's completely and absolutely dominant. We've just bought a new house and he loved it. I agreed with him that we should buy it because I thought the garden would give him something to do for the rest of his life but I *believed* that. I wouldn't have said it if I hadn't thought so. It's really important that women speak their *minds*.'

Shakira and I discussed a mutual friend, who was currently suffering from bad migraines due, we thought, to never being able to say what she really wanted or how she felt.

'My mother died of cancer at 52. I believe it was because she was never allowed to speak her mind. A lot of illness comes from repression,' I added.

'Do you know how many women are not *allowed* to speak their minds, do you know how many there are?' Shakira said to me. 'That's why so many Indian women get breast cancer, because they *constantly* worry. When I have a massage I say screw it, I'm going to stay in, have my massage and just watch television. But so many women are not *allowed* to do that and they feel guilty if they do. I think many women over a certain age – over 40, or 50 – feel guilty if they take time for themselves.'

'The "C'mon you lazy slut what are you doing lying around doing nothing? syndrome,"' I said.

'But they *shouldn't* feel guilty because everybody's pulling at them,' Shakira said. 'The husband wants something, the kids want

something, or their mother. Somehow you *have* to be in charge of so many people's lives that you forget what you *really* want or what you really *like*. I remember when we moved back here from LA to live, I had a bad sore throat for six months. One day I analysed the reason. I didn't know what was going on in my life. I thought I was going mad because I woke up every morning with a sore throat. Then I realised it was purely a physical reaction to what was going on in my life.'

'It was psychosomatic. Because you didn't know what was happening your body rebelled. I believe that when we're *really* ill it's because our bodies are saying we can't cope with any more stress,' I said.

'Always,' said Shakira.

'Today everyone goes through so much stress in life. Stress from the traffic, having to travel on crowded public transport, as well as the stress of simply walking down the street and encountering insulting strangers,' I said.

'That could put you off for the whole day. If I get into a cab and happen to have a rude cab driver I feel my whole day is wrecked. First thing in the morning, if Michael's in a bad mood I just stay out of the way – I must start off the day calmly.'

'It's terribly important how you start the day. What I want to do in the morning is drink a huge mug of coffee, read the papers and not talk much until I'm awake and balanced.'

'We all have our different ways of survival. If you survive and thrive day to day, you're okay, you're pretty strong,' said Shakira.

Shakira's innate calm and inner and outer serenity should be a lesson to us. I have never seen her upset, angry or in any way unbalanced even though she leads an extraordinarily full and active life. Byron could have written of her:

She walks in beauty, like the night
Of cloudless climes and starry skies;
And all that's best of dark and bright

DIAHANN
CARROLL

TELEVISION'S FIRST
BLACK BITCH

Diahann Carroll and I live in the same Los Angeles apartment building, a 1960s high-rise with a spectacular view from the beach to down town LA. I'd known and admired Diahann for over twenty years and we both bitched together in *Dynasty*, when she was proud to become 'Television's First Black Bitch'. Although our scenes were full of jealousy and spite we developed a tremendous rapport and our friendship grew stronger.

Diahann is a star in a tough business where to survive as a woman of colour and a woman of a certain age one needs the resiliency and hide of an ox. During Diahann's night-club act as the ultimate Diva she stands looking ravishing in a low-cut gown with great bones, perfect skin and toned body and tells the audience that she is 63. This always elicits a standing ovation as she is indeed wonderful looking. She seems to have no visible wrinkles and her effervescent personality and slightly self-mocking persona only add to her charm.

Carol Diahann Johnson was born in a poor district of Brooklyn in July 1935. Her parents doted on their beautiful eldest child, calling her 'Our Little Princess of Harlem'. Even at 5, Diahann had a cupboard crammed with dozens of beautiful dresses and was encouraged to be 'special, perfect, and pretty'.

Her mother Mabel often wrapped her daughter's hair in brown paper 'curlers' to give her fashionable Shirley Temple ringlets, and spent hours fussing with her curls, putting Diahann's hair bow in just the right place for maximum effect. But the family were also strict disciplinarians, insisting on regular church going, piano lessons and no loitering in the dangerous streets.

At age 15, Diahann was discovered by *Ebony* magazine and having won a talent competition changed her name to Diahann Carroll and got a job as a show girl at a glamorous Latin Quarter night club in New York. There she met the notorious Scandinavian transsexual Christine Jorgenson.

'Christine taught me a lot about how to talk, to move and to dress like a beautiful woman,' says Diahann. 'Who better to teach you *that* than a man who has been studying women and masquerading as one all his life?'

At 18 Hollywood beckoned and she played a supporting role in *Carmen Jones* with Harry Belafonte, the dazzlingly handsome calypso star.

'I fell madly in love with her,' says Belafonte. 'She was beautiful and talented, with a great voice.'

But Diahann was feisty, too, as Marlon Brando found out, when she rejected his amorous advances with a slap on the face.

Her Broadway star started to rise when she starred in *House of Flowers* singing the unforgettable 'When A Bee Lies Sleeping' then, before she was 21, the media discovered her and Diahann became the toast of New York.

She married Monte Kaye, a good-looking jazz impresario, gave birth to a baby girl, Suzanne, and was idyllically happy for several years. But her happiness was transitory and with passion came heartache. Diahann embarked on a long-term romance with married Sidney Poitier and divorced Monte Kaye amicably, but after nine years with Poitier, his reluctance to marry ended their relationship.

However, her career was far from over. Having won a Tony Award for *No Strings*, Diahann Carroll became the first female black television star in *Julia*, a number one show for three years. But alas, the gruelling schedule saw her in hospital for stress and in 1968 *Julia* ended. Undeterred, Diahann bounced back, regained her health and became engaged to television personality David Frost.

'I was madly in love with David,' says Diahann. 'But I gave him up because I loved him *too* much and I knew I wasn't what he really needed.'

She then accepted the challenging title role

in *Nadine*, a gritty, hard-edged movie about a Harlem woman single-handedly bringing up six children.

'Everyone thought I wouldn't be able to cut it,' she says. 'They thought I was too glamorous to be believable in that part – but I proved them wrong.' Diahann was Oscar nominated and again her career was back on track, making movies, giving concerts and going the night club route.

But tragedy struck when her husband of two years was killed in his Ferrari. Diahann was devastated and found herself in her early forties, unable to get work for the first time ever. Forgotten by Hollywood and in debt, it was the lowest ebb of her life.

But Diahann was nothing if not indomitable and in 1983 while watching *Dynasty* she thought '*That's* where I want to be and that's where I'm *going* to be.'

She arranged to sing at a party given by *Dynasty's* producer, Aaron Spelling, charmed the pants off him and convinced him that she should be part of the *Dynasty* team. Although she was completely different from what Aaron had envisaged in the role, Diahann was cast as Dominique Devereaux, Blake Carrington's dominating half-sister. 'I wanted to be the first black bitch on TV,' says Diahann gleefully. 'Strong, demanding and giving as good as she gets.'

Diahann pulled out all the stops in *Dynasty*. I know because I was right alongside her pulling 'em out too. Our sizzling fight scenes became legendary, and Nolan Miller worked overtime creating our outrageously over-the-top outfits.

Since *Dynasty* ended Diahann's star has continued to rise. She married entertainer Vic Damone, touring with him in a successful night-club act until they divorced in 1996, and is now at the peak of her career. Having played Norma Desmond in *Sunset Boulevard,* Diahann has launched her own line of clothing, wigs, jewellery, lingerie and handbags and is the first black female celebrity to have her own line. 'But I won't be the last,' she laughs.

Says Harry Belafonte, 'Had it not been for

The Battle of the Bitches, Dynasty, 1987.

Diahann, black actresses would not be perceived as favourably as they are today.'

Diahann Carroll endures, for she *never* takes NO for an answer.

IN BLACK PINSTRIPE TROUSERS, a simple white cotton shirt tied casually at the waist and wearing little make-up Diahann greeted me in her apartment. We both sipped Evian water as I asked her if she followed any special diet. She said that she didn't believe in diets but that her doctor advised her that the healthiest thing for her is absolutely no caffeine, no chocolate, no dairy products and no sodas or fizzy drinks.

I concurred with her about the fizzy drinks, then remembered that she loved champagne.

'Ah, but that's different,' Diahann smiled mischievously. 'I drink champagne every once in a while because it is *so* good for the soul. I believe it cleanses the mind and relaxes the nervous system, as does wine.'

'I agree with you about wine,' I said. 'The French drink tons of wine, and in general they're much slimmer as a race than Americans, and it's recently been proved that they're healthier, too.'

'Probably because they don't snack,' said Diahann.

'Do you snack?' I asked.

Diahann laughed. 'I don't believe in snacking but oh boy it's *hard*. It's better to have little meals several times a day. I don't always have breakfast, but if I do, I want a *big* breakfast. I'll have juice, squeezed grapefruit is best, with a little orange in it, but it must be freshly squeezed and drunk *immediately*. If I'm really

good I'll have half a grapefruit and a little honey, then for the rest of my meals I'll eat more or less what I want but *NOT too much*.'

'One of the best exercises I know for losing weight is the table exercise,' I said. 'You push yourself away from the table after eating only half of what is on your plate.'

'I'll try that,' she smiled.

'You have such good skin. Any secrets if one has dry skin?' I asked.

'My skin has a tremendous tendency to dry. Years ago I went to see *the* skin doctor to all the young models. He told me to put a quart of milk in my bath, not too much water, and a few drops of vegetable oil – sesame, apricot, anything that is as natural as possible. I tried it and it worked, so that's my secret. I was raised on the East Coast, where it's so cold in the winter that one needs to replenish the natural oils that are taken out of your skin.'

It's obviously working for Diahann because her skin looks glowing. Her daily skin care regime is also careful, and elaborate.

'I put on a little sunscreen, then I put on moisturiser and then I apply my make-up.'

'That's *exactly* what I do! And I'm sure you're scrupulous about removing it too.'

'I learned years ago that you must *never* under any circumstances sleep in your make-up. I don't care *what* has happened that evening!' She gave a sly little giggle. 'You must remove it, even if you put it on early in the morning so you look dewy on the pillow.'

'People say some actresses have bad skin because they sleep in their make-up,' I said.

'It's nice to wake up in the morning looking

'I've exercised all my life, maybe not as much as now, but I've always known that gravity was going to work against me one day so I wanted to give myself as much help as I could.'

good, but if you leave make-up on pores become clogged and they can't breathe when you are asleep.'

'What about night cream? Do you put anything on your face while you're sleeping?' I asked.

'Oh I do. I use one called La Mer that I like very much and my moisturiser is also by La Mer. In fact I use La Mer for everything, on my body too. If I'm going through a particularly dry skin period I smother Vitamin E oil on my skin.'

'But it's so thick and greasy.'

'I know and it takes forever to put on, but it's worth it. After I rub it in, I cover everything on my bed with towels, then go to sleep. I may do that twice a month if I'm in a dry climate and believe me it works. The elements are very destructive to the skin, so I always wear make-up outdoors for protection.'

'I know we both believe in that,' I said. 'I remember that *enormous* make-up bag you used to carry around on *Dynasty*. It weighed about thirty pounds and had everything in it. Do you ever go without make-up?'

'Occasionally I'll run around without it because once in a while the skin needs to breathe.'

'Have you noticed that most women over 45 who haven't protected their skin have a lot more wrinkles than those who've always used either moisturiser or make-up?'

Diahann agreed. 'Absolutely. It *is* boring and time consuming to put on, but then so is shaving.'

'Tell me about your exercise regime, Diahann. You do exercise – I've seen you.'

Diahann let out a huge sigh. 'It has to be – it has to be. I work out in the gym here with my trainer. We do our 45 minutes, then the treadmill for a half hour and that's it. I've exercised all my life, maybe not as much as now, but I've always known that gravity was going to work

against me one day so I wanted to give myself as much help as I could.'

I noticed her toned arms and asked if she worked out with weights.

'Since the arms don't do exactly what we want them to do we have to make them obey.' She pinched her upper arm. 'It's *this* area that wants to be naughty, and lifting weights can really tighten up the upper arms. But unless you've done it regularly you can't panic at 60 and undo all the damage. You need to start in your forties or younger.'

'Do you think that sleep is important for beauty?' I asked her. 'How many hours do you need?'

'I'm a disaster without it, an absolute *disaster*. It's not always the actual sleep I need but I *must* lie prone and comfortable. I like seven hours minimum. Even if I don't sleep, I want seven hours, either reading or watching TV.'

'So basically you're in bed for seven hours a night. Not counting horizontal jogging.' I said.

'Now *that's great* beauty therapy,' she smiled. 'Being in love.'

'So are you?' I asked.

'Joan *really*!' she laughed. 'Damone and I divorced last year and it was very stressful. There's no one on the horizon right now I'm sorry to say – but I don't rule it out.'

'You certainly live a stressful life,' I said. 'When you were doing *Sunset Boulevard*, your days must have been extremely hard. Did all that pressure affect your looks?'

Diahann sighed and sipped some Evian. 'When I see photos of me after my first eight months in *Sunset Boulevard* I cannot *believe* what I looked like. Not only *was* I exhausted but I looked it too. I think the pressure of a demanding role and not wanting to disappoint a bunch of people really took an incredible toll on me. Eight performances a week and being away from home for such a long period, it was hell.'

'I don't know *how* you walked up that stair-case in those heavy beaded gowns – they must have weighed 40 pounds each.'

'At *least*. I went up 729 stairs every perfor-mance *eight times a week*. And the terrible thing is that it affected the joint of my knee. When I had any free time I was at the gym working on this little muscle so that I wouldn't have a knee problem.' She touched behind her knee. 'It's still a bit painful.'

'How would you de-stress when the work-load became too heavy?'

'During *Julia* dancing and discotheques saved my life. I was younger then, but after a certain amount of dancing you don't care about anything except going home at night and falling asleep. Now I go home and just try and *rest*,' she smiled. 'I read and watch boring TV – that's great for sending you to sleep.'

'If you could take just one thing – one cos-metic or beauty ingredient – to a desert island, what would it be?'

'One thing?' She thought for a moment. 'Hmm. Bottled water.'

'Oh, too boring, darling. Something more *tangible*.'

'A man!' She laughed. 'A sexy one who is *very* self sufficient. And virile.'

'Okay, I'll let you have him,' I said. 'Now – the $64,000 question: do you believe in cos-metic surgery?' I asked.

'Oh yes, *absolutely*. I've had it and any actress or singer who looks good over a certain age who's said she hasn't is *lying*.' Diahann grinned widely and walked around her spa-cious living room, flexing her toned arms. 'Anything that makes you happier about your-self is something that you should do. If a per-son's livelihood is racing Ferraris, they have to send their Ferrari in for servicing. It's the same with one's looks if you're an entertainer. I don't care how much we exercise, how many creams we use, there are certain areas we are *not* going

to improve. However, I do think there's such a thing as overdoing cosmetic surgery.'

'There are too many quack surgeons out there,' I said. 'I've seen some *horrible* face-lifts in this town, but the worst one is that Bride of Wildenstein woman in New York.'

'Yes – she is freakish. It's sad. She's had so much done she looks like a gargoyle. But if your looks are your living and if you can afford it, do it. There are very few actors and actresses in this town who haven't had it done. We're so fortu-nate today to be able to take a couple of weeks off for surgery and reclaim five or even ten years. It's like fine tuning. After all, if there's something wrong with your heart doctors say "we can fix this valve" and of course you'll do it. However if you don't *have* to, if part of your life isn't your looks, then it doesn't matter. If you live in a place where no one has had plastic surgery and everyone's ageing the same way then don't even think about it. But I live between one coast and the other and I don't know *anyone* who's not been involved in some sort of cosmetic plastic surgery, and hurrah for them.'

'Do you think that positive thinking has a lot to do with the fact that you and I have sur-vived in this business, whereas hundreds of others of our era have fallen by the wayside?' I asked.

'Without a doubt. When I graduated from high school I didn't wait five minutes before I was in show business, because that was my dream. I *believe* in positive thinking, along with a good sense of humour. Every once in a while when I have taken myself too seriously I'll say, "Oh Diahann, you're such a bore, chill out girl".'

'Boring? I've never seen that side of you. *Never*.'

'It happens every once in a while, then I remind myself of all the wonderful, incredible things in my life and all the things that I can

'A woman is like a tea-bag. It's only when she's in hot water that you realise how strong she is.'

Photographed outside Spago restaurant, LA, 4 February 1998.

look forward to and hope for. Strong people are what we want to be, but it takes will-power to be that strong.'

'Nancy Reagan, who's also a strong woman, once said: "A woman is like a tea-bag. It's only when she's in hot water that you realise how strong she is",' I remarked.

Diahann laughed. 'I like that. Nancy's a gutsy lady.'

I asked her if she thought that attitudes had changed towards older women in recent years.

'Yes, I do,' she said vehemently. 'We are *so* different from our mothers. It's no longer "Oh she's 40, she's past her prime". In my mother's and grandmother's day at 40 you were definite-

ly *finished*. It's not true at all today. We are living in a very healthy time. I take the kind of vitamins that my mother had never *heard* of, and exercising and the awareness of our diets has also changed what we look like.'

'I know. I have photographs of my mother in her mid-forties and she looked older than I do now,' I said.

'My mother comments on it *constantly*,' said Diahann. 'She'll say to me, "I did not look the way you look at your age – you're not getting older, you're getting better".'

I told her I thought that her face and bone structure were much finer today than when she was in her twenties and thirties and asked her about vitamin supplements.

'Vitamin E of course, beta carotene, one multi-vitamin and vitamin C. *Every* day.'

'Are you into HRT?' I asked.

'Of *course*,' she answered. 'I'll go for anything that works. I find that HRT is really beneficial, not just for bones and skin but also for vitality. I feel healthy all the time, touch wood, but I really think a lot of that is attitude.'

'I agree,' I said. 'I know it's the attitude – plus the belief. Feel great and you'll look great; feel young, look young; feel intelligent and bright and you *are* intelligent and bright.'

'You know, Joan, when we were in our twenties and thirties we had everything going against us. I *do* have a reputation for being opinionated and pushy but that is about *survival*. I *am* opinionated. Why shouldn't I be? In my business I *know* what's best for me. How do you move forward up to the next rung without being opinionated?'

'True. You *have* to stick up for yourself even if that's not how you were brought up. I come from a generation in which my mother and all my female relations were completely subservient to their men.'

'I saw that in my relatives too and I didn't admire it. Our generation had to fight. We were brought up to be nice, good little girls then along came the 60s and the bra burning and the *Me* Generation – *I'm* going to have therapy and find myself, *I'm* not going to stay at home and

just raise babies. I felt that about myself and *you* felt that about yourself too.'

'But we had to re-think *everything* we'd been indoctrinated with,' I said. 'All that stuff about the female is the weaker sex, therefore the inferior sex, we had to expunge that from our conscious minds, it was starting anew.'

'Right,' agreed Diahann. 'And making the career versus motherhood choice. Women were *expected* to be mothers whether they wanted to be or not. I don't put homemaking *down*, but I believe you have to *know* if that is what's going to make you happy.'

'Hear! hear!' I said. 'Many women's lives are completely bound up with their families but parenthood goes so *fast*. I look back on raising my children and it seemed to pass in a flash.'

'Your relationship with your kids was always something I admired,' said Diahann. 'They *knew* that you were always there for them, even when you were working and that they could count on you. That's important when you have offspring. Giving from your experience, your life, your heart and soul.'

'Were you able to pass on to Suzanne, your daughter, your own experience of life?' I asked.

'Not everyone has the kind of curiosity I have about roaming the world and going places and doing things. She wasn't as interested in it as I was.'

'Do you believe that today in the 90s there are heroines? Did you have any when you were younger, and who are your heroines now?'

Diahann thought for a moment. 'Hillary Clinton. I admire her silence. It's incredible that she has held on to her dignity and her silence for so long. It seems she's made up her mind that *whatever* happens to her husband she will give everyone the impression that she is supportive of him. I think that's admirable. Mother Theresa. And of course Princess Diana. It's incredible that after her separation this

> **'I do have a reputation for being opinionated and pushy but that is about survival.'**

young woman said, "I am not going home to hide – I'm coming out and I'm coming out full force and I will have a *life. No one* is going to make me feel that I don't deserve my life. *Yes*, I made a mistake with my marriage, but I'll correct it with dignity and I shall find myself in areas that are humanitarian."'

Diahann looked sad. 'I admired her tremendously, too,' I said, then thought it was time to change subjects.

'You were twice voted one of the best dressed women in the world, so what is the secret of being well-dressed today? Were the rules different in the 50s, 60s and 70s?'

'For the most part it really hasn't changed *that* much,' said Diahann. 'Every woman should have a three-way mirror, it's essential. Stand in front of that mirror and ask and answer yourself as *honestly* as possible what *can* I wear and what must I *never* wear because it doesn't work for me. A dress may be all the rage but if it doesn't flatter *me* I won't wear it. You must accentuate your good features. I like to call attention to the fact that I am tall, and that I have long legs. For me less is *always* more. Less, less, less. Always remember that the mirror will *not* lie to *you*.'

'You're always glamorous, even when I saw you at the studio at five in the morning. I can't ever *imagine* you in a track suit and sneakers.'

'I wore them for a while in Palm Springs because all my friends were wearing them. Then an Italian man came over and told us, "You all look horrible in this little ugly uniform." I looked at us and he was right, we were clones, so I threw them away.'

'One obvious thing about you, Diahann, is that you really know who you are and what you want.'

'You'd better believe it. If I haven't got it together by my age then I might as well give up.' Diahann jumped up and stretched. 'Okay. Work over now, it's time for a glass of champagne.'

WE TOASTED EACH OTHER and I smiled. 'As one Queen Bitch to the other, darling, long may you reign.'

A few weeks later, during a routine examination Diahann found a small lump in her breast. I called to commiserate and she said:

'It was a shock. I just went in for a routine check-up and they said they had to investigate. It was frightening. The waiting was terrible, especially those days in between when you can't tell anyone because you don't want to worry them. So you sit and you wait and worry on your own.'

In May, Diahann underwent successful surgery to remove the cancerous growth, and following six weeks of radiation treatment her doctors now expect a full recovery.

'I have to say I feel blessed that they found it in time and were able to take care of it immediately,' Diahann said. 'That's why I'm going public, to help other women and remind them to monitor themselves. I can't emphasise strongly enough how important it is for women to pay close attention to their bodies and medical needs and take control of their health, by getting examined regularly. The phone calls have been non-stop. People have reached out in such a loving way. I've never been part of a Hollywood scene, so this is wonderful. I am somewhat fatigued, but other than that, I feel fine. The doctors tell me that after five or six weeks of radiation treatment, I'll be able to resume my work schedule with no alteration in my plans. I'm going to bore everyone to death now with the importance of checking your breasts regularly. Early detection saved my life and illness brings your life into perspective. Cancer isn't glamorous, but it is *important* that people realise that celebrities don't have an exemption from reality.'

Diahann Carroll – Survivor and Diva Supreme.

Photographed by Eddie Sanderson at Doubles Club, Sherry Netherlands Hotel, New York City, 5 May 1998.

ARLENE DAHL

THE BEAUTIFUL GURU

ELEGANT AND BEAUTIFUL, Arlene Dahl has, with good reason, become a beauty guru for millions of women. She has written sixteen books on health, beauty and astrology which have offered unique all-encompassing approaches to both inner and outer happiness and loveliness. Arlene still has the most extraordinary flawless white skin, dazzling blue-green eyes and brilliant Viking-red hair, inherited from her Norwegian ancestors. At 5'7" her 138 pounds is exceedingly well distributed and it's hard to believe that she's 70, with a modelling and film career that spans five decades. Arlene has three children and several grandchildren. Her eldest son is Lorenzo Lamas, by the handsome actor Fernando Lamas.

An actress since the 1940s, Arlene Dahl has starred in twenty-eight films, two television series and dozens of plays. She has been a successful designer, internationally syndicated beauty and astrology columnist and in 1970 she was chosen as Woman of the Year.

I first saw Arlene in Hollywood in the late 50s. I was under contract to 20th Century-Fox and she was on the lot shooting *Journey to the Centre of the Earth* with James Mason. It was a baking-hot California day and as I walked barefaced and bare-shouldered across the studio lot, still unaware of the potential damage the sun could wreak, a vision came gliding towards me. Arlene Dahl was as exquisite as a porcelain doll in a period costume that accentuated her beautiful figure. But what struck me the most was that she carried a parasol to protect her perfect pale complexion from the harsh rays. Arlene was aware of the sun and its deadly effect long before anyone else.

FORTY YEARS LATER WE meet for lunch on a cold and rainy May day in Doubles, a New York club of which Arlene is a member. She looked *soignée* in a brown coat and boots, her pale red hair immaculately coiffed, her magnolia skin as flawless as ever. After ordering a light lunch my opening question had to be what was the secret of her perfect skin?

'I went to Florida when I was 17. My mother had always told me the sun was bad but I didn't listen. I was determined to get a tan so I covered myself in oil and got absolutely *fried*! I was so seriously ill that I was hospitalised for two weeks and the doctor said: "If you get through this without scars, you must *never* go in the sun again, you are allergic to it." So mother was right. Luckily I didn't scar, but I learned that lesson early in life.'

'Lucky for you,' I said. 'So what's your beauty routine today?'

'I believe what you put *into* your body is just as important as what you put *on* it. I don't wear any foundation unless I'm on the screen.'

Journey to the Centre of the Earth, *1959*.

'The value of exercise cannot be overestimated. Use it or lose it.'

I looked at her astonishing skin and said I found it hard to believe.

'I moisturise, of course, and touch up any marks with a brush and Bobby Brown concealer. Then I brush on Elizabeth Arden translucent powder, which is getting harder and harder to find because all the manufacturers are putting colour in their powders now.'

'It looks as though you're wearing perfect matte make-up with no foundation,' I said.

'Foundation clogs the pores. When I was making my first movie test, I wore Max Factor, which was murder because I'm allergic to most make-up. My face blew up before the test take and I almost didn't make it in films because I couldn't take the make-up. Then Perc Westmore at Warner Brothers made a special non-allergic make-up for me which only Ingrid Bergman and I wore. It had an oil base and was like an all-day beauty treatment, so even though the lights were hot it protected your skin.'

'What else do you do for your skin?'

'It's quite dry so I've concocted a special mixture. Beat two eggs thoroughly and apply the mixture to your face and neck. Rest for twenty minutes until the mix hardens, then wash it off. You'll be amazed how refreshed your complexion looks. For dry skin use *only* the egg yolk, thoroughly beaten.'

'I'll try it,' I said and then asked Arlene if she exercised.

'The value of exercise cannot be overestimated,' said Arlene vehemently. 'Use it or lose it. Walking is one of the best forms of exercise. Get a dog. Two or three times a week get yourself to a gym, or go to a personal trainer. I use 21b and 51b weights on my legs and wrists to increase bone density when I'm exercising.'

'And do you diet?' I asked.

'I believe in healthy food, and would *never* crash diet. It ruins the skin and causes stretch marks. Health is *vital* to beauty. Vitamins, exercise and eating properly are three major priorities. Women over 40 should definitely have vitamin C, E and calcium, take multi-vitamins at least once a day. What you put into your body is so important. Eat *fresh* fruit, have three balanced meals a day and if you must snack, make it healthy with an apple.'

'What was your philosophy in the last beauty book you wrote, *Beyond Beauty*?'

'Ideals of beauty change from year to year, decade to decade, but however they alter, one thing stays the same; you *have* to work at it. It's not easy, and the more you have to start with the more you have to lose.'

I told Arlene that she'd lost very little.

'It's discipline, what we were all trained to do in the 40s, 50s and 60s. Most young actresses today can't be bothered, so a lot of them look a mess. Models like Helena Christensen and Claudia Schiffer make sure they always look gorgeous. They know how to walk, how to stand, how to use their bodies. The ones who take acting classes even know how to act a little. This should be a lesson to actresses.'

The menu arrived and Arlene glanced at it then ordered a simple salad followed by chicken. I noticed she didn't wear glasses. She told me she'd been practising eye exercises which have improved her sight and which she will talk about in her next book, *Lasting Beauty.*

'You're such a positive person. Were you born with that?' I asked.

She nodded and I added, 'But obviously bad things happen to all of us!'

'We all have hills and valleys. But that's what life is, isn't it?' she said.

'Not a bowl of cherries, more a bowl of

cherry pips,' I said, and then asked her how she de-stressed and relaxed.

'I get on my portable slant board. Like the ones that we used at MGM. I have one in my office and one in my apartment. You can make one yourself easily enough, just get an ironing board and prop it up to about 30 degrees from the ground at one end and then lie down with your feet at the raised end for twenty minutes

and relax. The principle is to reverse the flow of blood – so you have to just lie there. Daily use of the slant board can *definitely* improve ageing skin and thinning hair. I do twenty minutes every morning. It reverses the circulation and nourishes the hair follicles. There'd be fewer bald people if they reversed their circulation – it fills the brain with blood. You *could* do it without a board, lying on the floor and elevating your feet 30 degrees. At night my bed is raised at the foot, and you sleep so much better. It makes sense to have your feet higher than your head.'

'That makes so much sense – I'm going to try it,' I said.

'I think pillows are bad. Sleeping on a soft pillow creates lines and destroys the chin line. I travel with my own beauty pillow like the Japanese – they use these bricks because of their elaborate hair dos. Japanese women have wonderful jaw lines and I believe it's the result of their brick training! Norma Shearer gave me this beauty secret a hundred years ago, when she told me to put a little baby pillow under the head, since that's the only place where you need support.' She indicated the back of her neck. 'You can buy them in the baby department, and I always travel with one.'

'What is your secret for getting rid of bags under the eyes, because you don't have any.' I enquired.

'Tea-bags. Put cold plain tea-bags on the eyes for eight minutes, then lie on the slant.'

'What do you do to relax?'

'Sleeping on a soft pillow creates lines and destroys the chin line.'

'I like to listen to beautiful music and I *love* to dance. Luckily so does my husband. They have dancing here every night with a live orchestra and we dance the night away. I like to dance so much I'll just put on music and dance with my dog if my husband isn't there,' she laughed.

I'd been out dancing with Arlene, so I knew how much fun she had. I turned to the question of heroines, and asked her whom she admired.

> ## 'Self-love has to come first, because unless you love yourself selfishly, you can't expect to love anyone else.'

'Barbara Cartland and Rose Sachs who's fantastic. She's an 80-year-old Southern Belle – always on the move. I think Rose feels if she stopped her life would stop and she's probably right. Once you stop contributing to life you stop living.'

'And once you stop learning you stop living,' I said. 'I telephoned Betsy Bloomingdale yesterday, who said "Darling, I can't talk to you now, I'm in the middle of my French lesson." When she called back I told her I thought it was admirable she was learning French and she said, "I believe that the brain is like a muscle that has to be exercised so you can continue to use it all your life."'

I asked Arlene what she thought was the most detrimental thing for beauty .

'Smoking,' she said vehemently. 'It causes deep wrinkles on your face and turns the face and teeth yellow.'

'If you could only take one inanimate thing to a desert island, what would it be?'

'Inanimate? I'd prefer something animate,' she laughed. 'But you know, Joan, I think the greatest beauty secret of *all* is love. To love and to be loved. A woman in love has a certain glow and that glow can also derive from the love she has for her children. The look is unmistakable. Self-love has to come first, because unless you love *yourself* selfishly, you can't expect to love anyone else. If you have children, you *must* love yourself in order to share that love with your children, and you must *teach* them love. Sharing love, whether it's physical or spiritual love or whether love of family and friends, you have to share – sharing should be the greatest source of love in your life. You and I have both been given a great deal in our life, but unless we share it we don't get the benefit.'

'I *totally* agree with that. We both know a lot of people who have tons of money, great houses and lovely things but don't share,' I said.

'It's sad to see people with lots of money, whether they made it or inherited it, who are stingy and mean,' she said.

'Do you believe that everything you put into life will eventually reward you? That if you're bad, it will all come back?'

'*Absolutely*,' said Arlene. 'There's an old saying, "Everything that you send into the lives of others, comes back into your own" and that means the good *and* the bad.'

'Then I'm going to be very, *very* good from now on,' I smiled.

Arlene, who is on her fourth marriage and very happy, made a toast: 'To love.' We laughed and clinked our glasses of wine and I said, 'the biggest beauty secret of them all.'

ANGIE DICKINSON

SEASONED SEX-SYMBOL

ANGIE DICKINSON'S LIFE AND career has been rich and fulfilling for over four decades. Discovered by a talent scout in a beauty contest, then spotted by Howard Hawks in the 50s for a starring role opposite John Wayne in *Rio Bravo*, international stardom and pin-up-hood soon followed. She starred in *The Bramble Bush* with Richard Burton, *Sins of Rachel Cade* with Peter Finch and Roger Moore, *Captain Newman, M.D.*, with Gregory Peck, *The Killers* with Lee Marvin, *The Chase* with Marlon Brando, *Oceans Eleven* with Frank Sinatra, and many others.

Angie became as well known for her inviting all-American sexuality, which she used to maximum effect both on and off screen, as for her movies. During the 60s and 70s she became a grown-up sex symbol, which culminated in

Photographed by Eddie Sanderson at Joan's LA apartment, 26 May 1998, with the 'Lady Joan' sculpture.

her starring as fiery Sgt Pepper Anderson in the hit television series *Policewoman*. This brought Angie international acclaim and a series of awards, including the Golden Globe for Best Actress, two Lead Actress Emmy nominations and many awards and citations from civic and police groups for her portrayal of a policewoman.

I met Angie when I was cast as a neurotic movie star (*not* type casting thank you!) in one of *Policewoman*'s episodes, curiously called *Trick Book*. We hit it off so well that, six months later, she asked me to guest again.

I admired her strong work ethic, down to earth humour and just plain *niceness* – an unusual quality for Hollywood actresses starring in their own series. Half the crew were in love with her, she performed many of her own stunts, and the most frequently used adjective to describe her was 'adorable'.

After four years as America's best known policewoman, Angie returned to features as a suburban housewife with erotic fantasies in the suspense thriller, *Dressed To Kill*, with Michael Caine.

Angie was born in Kulm, North Dakota, where her parents owned and operated a weekly newspaper. When she was 10, they moved to California where Angie attended parochial schools, then Glendale College. For a short time she worked in an aircraft parts plant to finance her acting lessons.

She married the brilliant composer Burt Bacharach in 1965, but divorced in 1982. They have one daughter, Nikki, who is their pride and joy. Rumours have been rife for years that Angie had a long-term affair with President John Kennedy, which she has always resolutely neither confirmed nor denied, but it's no secret that she and Frank Sinatra were an item for quite a while after *Oceans Eleven*. A strong friendship developed both with Sinatra and his wife Barbara, which has continued.

On the day we were supposed to meet Angie telephoned to say she didn't think she could make it, because she was still devastated by Sinatra's death four days previously. However, like the pro she is, Angie pulled herself together and arrived at my LA apartment carrying 'Lady Joan' in a large sack. This was a carved glass statue of a beautiful naked woman that I had given her, and I was amazed that she'd lugged it all the way from her place to mine.

'I wanted you to see she was still in one piece in spite of the earthquake,' laughed Angie. 'She's still got pride of place in my house.'

We settled down in my living room with cups of tea and I asked her about her beauty routine.

'If I have any beauty routine at all, it's smiling,' she smiled. 'But one must be smiling from *within*. I believe that the muscles of smiling and lifting are part of the luck that comes with having good bone structure. I've seen many pictures of myself, and when I'm not smiling I look totally different; drawn, angry, hard. After a certain age one's face tends to look stern if one doesn't smile, because we don't have that soft roundness that we had when we were kids. My face was very round when I was 12, because I was quite pudgy.'

'You were *never* pudgy Angie!'

'I was – I was called Beef Truss at school. But it was just adolescent fat which I lost. I do love to eat and right now I'm 20 pounds overweight. I'm heavy because I eat too much. The one comforting thing is that you know you can take it off,' she said.

'Except that it gets much more difficult as you get older,' I said. 'How would you advise a teenager to lose weight?'

'Well, when I got the part in *Rio Bravo* Hawks said, "You have a pretty good figure but it could be better. Go to that woman in the Valley" So I did. Louise Lang's diet was four days of two eggs for breakfast, lunch and dinner and half a grapefruit in the morning. At lunch you ate a tomato and half a grapefruit, and dinner was tomato and half a grapefruit and three cups of coffee and/or water maximum. That's *it*. So you lost a lot of water – but you also *lost* the weight. If you were going for a cover of a magazine or a movie casting, you were ready.'

'It sounds like a real crash diet. I went on one when I was at Fox, the banana and milk diet. But crash diets aren't the long-term answer for people who are seriously overweight, which you and I aren't,' I said.

Angie sighed. 'It's not easy anymore. It used to be, but now I don't have the will-power. I gain the most weight when I eat breakfast, so I try to eliminate it and eat an early lunch. I make a really wonderful tuna salad. Lettuce, cucumbers, tomato, celery, maybe avocado. Avocado's fattening but it's so rich in nutrients,' she said.

'Do you drink wine?' I asked.

'I don't drink much of *anything*, so if I give up wine it isn't that much of a help. But if you drink a lot of wine and you stop *then* you notice it,' she said. 'As one gets older, the face gets haggard if you lose too much weight. If we're too thin the arms and legs look bad.'

I asked her if she thought skincare was important.

'Definitely. I clean my face thoroughly every night with cleanser or a cold cream, and then clean it *again* and see what I missed and how much didn't come off. I *always* follow with astringent, then I'll find *more* that didn't come off. It sounds like I wear a ton of make-up, and I do,' she giggled, 'but I feel I look *better* with it. I wear a *lot* of eye make-up, and whatever else I want. I don't *care* what's in fashion – women should fix themselves up as they like to look. I've always worn make-up during the day, even though I love to give my face a rest and say ah, today is my day off. So my face can rest, I don't put *anything* on. If somebody shows up, then I run for the hat and the dark glasses – I have very blonde eyelashes and very dark hair under this blonde – I bleach everything that's dark and I dye everything that's blonde.' She gave a juicy laugh.

'After a certain age one's face tends to look stern if one doesn't smile, because we don't have that soft roundness that we had when we were 12.'

'I never knew you were a brunette,' I said. 'My true colour was in *Rio Bravo*,' she smiled. 'Because Barbara Rush was brunette the producers of *The Bramble Bush* said they couldn't have another brunette, because the audience couldn't know one from the other – the old-fashioned way of thinking – so they blonded me up and that was that.'

'Is colouring bad for your hair?' I asked.

'Oh yes, it's *terrible.*'

'Your hair is very fine,' I remarked.

'There's *nothing* finer than mine. It's baby hair, so I wear wigs sometimes. I wouldn't be without a wig – when I'm travelling for those television shows at seven o'clock in the morning. Sometimes people say, "You're wearing a wig" and I say no, *yesterday* was a wig, today's

my real hair! But I don't care, the main thing is I don't have time; fixing hair is terribly time-consuming.'

'Don't I know it. And it never lasts – mine always flops.'

'I pulled up outside your building, there was a gust of wind and my set was gone!' she laughed.

I asked her philosophy of life and Angie explained:

'I look at all the problems I could have and don't. Somebody said to my ex-husband once, how come Angie smiles so much? It was meant as a criticism of course, but I thought, what do I *not* have to smile about? I'm *not* ill, my child is well and I have a good job, an income and no huge tragedy has struck me. I believe that people should be very humble and grateful for the good fortune they've had. It all comes back to the smiling and the happy countenance within,' she said.

'Do you believe that one gets the face that one deserves?' I asked.

'Oh yes. You're a happy soul Joan, so when you walk in a room you're bright and proud. Geminis do that. Gemini lights up the world.'

'Are you Gemini?' I asked.

'No, I wish I were. I'm a Libra. There is no one good sign, but Gemini are a bright sign, there's no question. Libras are pretty "up" and that's a gift from God, because we can't choose that.'

I poured more tea, then I asked Angie how she de-stressed.

'My favourite way to relax is Solitaire. I adore cards and I love poker best of all,' she said. 'Do you remember, I played with you and Warren in the early 60s? I love the manipulation of cards. People scoff and say why not play Solitaire on a computer? But I say I can't *shuffle* a computer, I love to shuffle cards, and handling them keeps my hands working. I started Solitaire for my brain. My sister has had Alzheimer's for fifteen years and since she's only two years older than I, I started checking my own brain. Solitaire is a *great* brain exercise and it has helped the arthritis in my hands.'

'Scientists are discovering that if people don't use their brains, just sit and watch TV all day, once past 50 or 60, their brain starts to atrophy,' I said.

'I have *no* doubt about it,' agreed Angie. 'You *must* exercise and stimulate the brain.'

I mentioned that taking cider vinegar once a day with honey was supposed to be good for arthritis and Angie resolved to try it.

When I asked Angie the desert island question, she replied:

'When I was younger I'd take mascara, now I'd say eyeliner because I feel completely naked without my eyes on,' she laughed.

'Women who are ball-breakers are not in for a good life.'

'Isabel Huppert was on TV the other day, with bright red lips, matching hair and not a *stitch* of eye make-up. It looked *too* weird,' I said.

'If you are young enough that's fine. But you and I created a beast, so we have to live up to our glamour image. Most of us who created a look – Elizabeth Taylor, Ursula Andress, Raquel Welch, Gina Lollabrigida – can't change that look and we'd look silly if we did.

When you finally *find* your look after 35 or 40, it's usually the best one,' said Angie.

I asked her if she had any heroines.

'I have three. Jacqueline Kennedy, Pamela Harriman and Gloria Vanderbilt. I love those women for their great style and their femininity and their *chutzpah*. They were *strong*, of course and they were beautiful too – the whole package.'

'I think there's nothing more pathetic than a woman of *un certain âge* trying to emulate the hair styles, make-up and clothes of 20-year-olds. It doesn't work. Goldie Hawn's about the only person I know who gets away with it.' Angie agreed and, with that, we moved onto a fresh subject.

'Do you want to talk about the man in your life right now?' I asked.

'Well, I like being with a man – but when *I* want to. Not steadily, because they get in the way and I need both closets!' We laughed and she said, 'Love is alive. I know everyone's raving about Viagra, but my friends and I are trying to get *less*, not more!'

'We wasted so much time in our 20s and 30s on love and romance. It was too time consuming,' I ruminated.

'I always wanted *romance*. If I had a crush on somebody he was all I could think about. It wasn't so much the act of sex as being with that man. I was sexual but the sexuality came *after* romance, which I think is the way my generation was,' Angie said.

'It was because of the guilt feelings that our mothers' generation laid on us. Good girls don't do that sort of thing. We rebelled, but we still only had sex *after* the chase,' I said.

'Now the *next* generation was the opposite. *First* you made love and *then* you fell in love. Because of the way you were brought up you waited till the last *second* to give in to the guy, and then when you were powerless you surrendered.' Angie gave a hearty giggle.

'Didn't you once say that you used to have the lights *on* and now you like the lights down?' I asked.

'Now I want them *off*,' she laughed. 'Definitely *off*. It used to depend on the man. I did what he liked. I could cope with anything he wanted; after all he's the one who leads the parade.'

'But Angie, it's considered so old-fashioned to think that,' I said.

'Well, that's too bad,' Angie smiled.

'Girls in their thirties today say *they* start the ball rolling, and they get annoyed if the ball isn't rolling in their court right away. It's the instant gratifaction society,' I said.

'There are an awful lot of pushy women today and I think it's a turn-off to a lot of men. Women who are ball-breakers are not in for a good life,' she said.

I asked Angie if she exercised and she shuddered.

'Not enough. I have all the equipment at home, so I do it two or three times a week. I have a walking machine, a bicycle, a treadmill and a rowing machine. I also do Pilates, which is fabulous. Pilates works *everything*. I don't do it *nearly* enough. I never believed in sit-ups. Louise thought it was bad for the female organs and not good for the back.'

'Do you think there comes a time when a woman should cover up?' I asked.

'Absolutely. This morning I went to read for a movie. The script said my character was in bed. I said, "Do you mean in the *bedroom* or in *bed*? Because if you consider me for this role, I want to wear a jacket," I said. I was trying to get across to him, that if he wanted me to wear a strapless thing, I wouldn't. If he knows it up front, then there are no problems. Anyway he didn't hire me and that's okay. It's impossible over 60, which I am, to look like a 30-year-old. Do I wish I could? Of *course* I do, but that's foolish.' She smiled and sipped her tea.

'I think it's more dignified to be more covered up as one gets older,' I said. 'If the face and hair look great, which yours do, I don't know or care what the rest of you looks like.'

'I'm not *trying* to look like I used to,' said Angie. 'I told my agent to remind them they're *not* going to see *Policewoman* Pepper walk in that door. Because I'll read for a certain role and realise they're trying to make me look 40, and I say I'm *not* 40. Don't even *send* me up for it. Accepting your age and the advantages and disadvantages is the only way.'

'There are many advantages which come with age – I'm much more patient, tolerant and understanding now,' I remarked.

'Oh my God yes. A hundredfold,' Angie agreed.

I asked her if she would ever quit working and she said:

'*No*, never. I work all the time. Even if I'm not on a project or a movie, it's a charity, or it's publicity, or it's a book. I *love* to work,' she said, 'And long may you continue,' I said.

We had our photos taken with 'Lady Joan' and then Angie had to leave to meet her daughter so we made plans to get together over the poker table in the autumn.

Angie Dickinson is truly terrific fun, a lady whom both men and women genuinely like and admire. At the door she turned smiling and said, 'You know what I say at the end of each day, Joan? "If it wasn't too bad a day, it was a *great* day!" '

And carrying 'Lady Joan', Angie walked into the hazy afternoon.

MORGAN

Photographed by Eddie Sanderson at Joan's LA apartment, 20 May 1998.

Petitely beautiful, with a doll-like face and figure and a great sense of fun, there's much more to gorgeous Morgan Fairchild than meets the eye. In addition to her accomplishments as an actress, Morgan is an outspoken and dedicated supporter of AIDS research, women's pro-choice movements, and a large range of environmental issues. Beneath the beautiful babe exterior lies a studious bookworm. For recreation Morgan likes nothing better than to read medical journals and books and visit science museums.

Born in Dallas in the 50s, Morgan began acting as a child, when her mother enrolled her in drama lessons because she was too shy to give a book report in class. From age 10 she performed in children's and dinner theatre and stock productions in Dallas. She landed a juicy role in *Search for Tomorrow,* a daily soap, six weeks after moving to New York, then moved to LA in the 1970s. Her career really took off when she played the key role of the bitchy Constance Weldon Carlyle in *Flamingo Road,* for which she was nominated for a Golden Globe for Best Actress. Since then she has starred in many more TV and stage productions, and recently won an Emmy for *Murphy Brown.*

I first worked with Morgan in 1984 when we were the distaff side of a high camp TV Special called *Blondes Versus Brunettes.*

Fifteen years later we had tea on a beautiful May afternoon in my LA apartment. We reminisced about that show and our parody of

FAIRCHILD
SCIENTIFIC BABE

'I think men are more threatened now, because they really don't know what to do if you're a glamorous and beautiful woman and you are at all smart. Sure, there are some men who appreciate us, but a lot of guys get intimidated.'

Dynasty; in one sketch she played a very convincing Alexis and I a passable Krystal. We were both 'glitzed' to the nines in flashy 80s style – baubles, beads and feathers everywhere. In contrast today Morgan's tailored orange Versace jacket and black pants and my beige suede shirt and trousers seemed laid back.

'You don't look any different since *Blondes Versus Brunettes*,' I told her. 'Your skin is still amazing. What's your beauty secret?'

'I *never* go in the sun. I guess I was fortunate, as when I was a teenager I didn't have the patience to sit in it! I started in the theatre when I was 10, going straight from school to the theatre. Weekends I'd have matinées, so when most teenagers were giving themselves skin damage I was always working,' she said.

'Do you use moisturiser?' I asked.

'Everything! I'll try *anything* known to science. I'm a science nut. I wanted to be a doctor or technologist when I was a kid, so I'm always reading about all the latest products that are coming out and trying to grasp the new technology. I'll try anything new – I use glycolic acid cream, with 15 per cent glycol, which is heavier than you'd get in a cream you buy at the department store, but I get it from my skin doctor and use it at night and it gets rid of surface blemishes. The hydroxy acids are good because they lift off the top layer of skin, then some of the retinoids, like Retinol, or Retin A are excellent. There are new ones being developed that will help to build collagen,' she said authoritatively.

I was hughly impressed by Morgan's knowledge and her scientific studies of skin. 'It obviously works,' I said. 'Of all the women I have talked to you have the best skin. Arlene Dahl has fabulous skin, too and she never went in the sun either.'

'I have very pale thin skin which is prone to get dry and wrinkle early *so* I'm *very* careful. I don't smoke, I don't drink, I *never* did drugs, and I'm probably the only person in my generation who never even had a puff on a joint! I try to keep up-to-date on all the scientific breakthroughs because, up until a few years ago, one cream or moisturiser was about the same as another. It was all in the marketing and packaging, but now there are all these new technologies, like liposomes, that can deliver deeper and better than they used to under the skin. There are also the retinoids which strengthen and the hydroxys which strip off a layer of skin. Of course, you have to be careful not to *over*-use skin preparations. Doctors are worried about the tendency to over-use alpha-hydroxys, because there's a *reason* skin builds up a layer – which is to protect it from the sun. They fear that women are stripping away all the top layers, which are the protective layers of skin, and exposing themselves to the risk of skin cancer,' she explained.

'So you believe in protecting your skin?' I asked.

'At *all* times,' Morgan said vehemently. 'It's essential for the sun. I'm so *white*. I'm like the whitest person on earth. I have white eye-lashes, white eyebrows. When I was a kid I was white-haired – if I don't have some colour on my face, I look like a cadaver.'

We both laughed and I told her I'd seen her without make-up and she looked great. 'Your eye make-up is fabulous. Do you put blue inside the eye?'

'That's one of my make-up tricks. I put navy blue on the inside of the eyelid and it makes your eyes look much bigger. Princess Diana used to do it. I love mascara. Because I have white eyelashes, without mascara I look like an newborn chicken.'

I noticed her hands were slightly tanned and asked if she put sun-bloc on them.

'Yes, sun-bloc under my make-up. The European ones are 60 SPF, as opposed to the 15 or 20 you find here, and are much better. Living in Southern California you've *got* to protect your skin as much as possible. Not only from wrinkles but also to prevent changes in pigmentation, another problem as you get older. You *have* to protect from skin cancer now. All of us have to be much more careful of the sun than a generation ago, for health reasons as opposed to just beauty reasons, because of the increasing damage to the ozone layer.'

'That's so terrifying,' I said. Then I asked her if she had a trainer.

'I had different trainers, but after a while I stopped using them – unless I'm training for something special, for example if I had to wear a bikini. God knows, at my age I would try to duck that like crazy.'

'Don't be ridiculous, your figure is fabulous!'

'I'm very disciplined because I started in the theatre so young. I try to exercise every day. That means I *don't* every day, but if you aim for every day, I end up doing it several times a week. I like different kinds of aerobics, either a cycle or a stairmaster or I love that new sort of pre-coursing, that's half-ski, half-cross country, half-stairmaster. It's very hard and it really burns me up. And then I work out on weights and go on the machines. For the deltoids I start with 5lbs then work up to 8lbs and do the biceps and triceps with 8lbs. I don't want to get bulky. I see too many girls in my gym who are too bulky. My body type is small so that's not really a problem, but something that I might have to face later, because muscle turns to fat. I don't want to get thick-looking, with big muscles.'

I asked her how she de-stressed and Morgan told me she produced a stress management video a few years ago. 'Stretching is really good. Ever since I was a kid, if I got upset I'd repeat this line like a mantra, "In the universal scheme of things, it really doesn't matter," and I'd just picture the universe with all the planets floating to put life in perspective. Our little day to day stresses don't really amount to a row of beans. I also practise Tai Chi, which is like Kung Fu in slow motion, and I do yoga, which has a different approach, it makes you concentrate on what you are doing and on particular muscles.'

Moving onto another topic I asked Morgan what she would take on a desert island.

'I'd take mascara because without eyelashes I have no colour. I need help there to give my face a little focus.'

Then I asked about her heroines and she answered, 'Marilyn Monroe, I liked her a lot, but I don't know if she's a heroine. Because I was always interested in science, I have different heroes. Pasteur was an idol of mine, and the early medical guys, Edward Jenner, who invented vaccination and Lister who discovered the benefits of antiseptics. So basically I admire various scientists and Marilyn. It's an odd collection.'

'It's certainly an eclectic one,' I said. 'I admired Marilyn too. She was a much better actress than people gave her credit for.'

'She was brilliant,' said Morgan. 'Watch *Some Like It Hot* or *Gentlemen Prefer Blondes* and the way she takes a *nothing* line and turns it into something hysterical. We know how

hard it is to carry off that effervescent character. Whenever you see somebody doing an imitation of Marilyn, it becomes heavy handed and tawdry and yet she made her characters seem *real*, they *existed*: dear, charming, funny and sweet, instead of just a cheap blonde stripper, which is all a lot of her imitators are.'

'Marilyn was the major sex goddess and icon of the 50s. Do you think people's attitude towards glamorous, beautiful women has changed since Marilyn's time?' I asked.

'In a funny way I think men are more threatened now, because they really don't know what to do if you're a glamorous and beautiful woman and you're at all smart. Sure, there are some men who appreciate us, but if you're bright and attractive, especially *glamorously* attractive as opposed to just attractive, a lot of guys get intimidated,' Morgan said.

'I've often been called a bitch, not just because of the roles I play but because I'm reasonably smart and outspoken. You've never been called a bitch, have you?' I asked.

'Occasionally,' she giggled. 'In our business if a woman stands up for herself at all, she's seen as difficult. Producers don't like actors making a stand on *anything* anyway, but if you're a male actor they think that you have integrity, and they give you credit for being an individual. If you're an actress and say 'I can't say this line' then you're a troublemaker.'

'Men still get away with murder,' I sighed. I poured some more tea and admired Morgan's new short hair cut. 'Don't you think women over 40 look better with shorter hair, they look more chic? It's a fresher, newer look,' I asked.

'I guess it's true. Not the day you *turn* 40 but as time goes on. Since I cut mine people keep saying "Oh you look so much younger." Not that they ever told me that I looked like hell before,' she laughed. 'I have thick, good hair to begin with. It's like a horse's tail. When I went to get it cut the first time it was down to my

'My basic philosophy of life is: life is a banquet and most poor suckers are starving to death.'

waist, the stylist pulled it back and held it and said, 'Blondes don't usually have thick or coarse hair. I've never seen a blonde with hair like that."

'Great hair, great skin – you've been lucky in many ways,' I said. 'What do you feel is the secret of a good life?' 'My basic philosophy of life is: life is a banquet and most poor suckers are starving to death.

'I always wanted my life to be a great adventure. I grew up in Dallas and my mother was an English teacher and my father was an engineer. I didn't fit in in high school. I wasn't interested in football or being a cheerleader. I was a very mature kid and my ambition was to not get stuck, living the boring life my parents lived. I wanted to travel. I wanted to do things. So many of the people I grew up with still live within three miles of the high school we went to, and their kids have graduated from the same high school. I wanted a chance to see everything and meet interesting people who didn't care about football.'

'How did you get into the theatre when you were 9, if your mother was a school teacher?' I asked.

'When I was in the fifth grade I was shy, incapacitatingly shy. I never opened my mouth, although I was in all the advance placement courses and got straight As. However, at the end of the year they put on a play and, being a starchy little person, I got to play the adult in the play. I found I didn't actually mind being on the stage, where you had a character to hide behind. Then my mother *made* me go to my first audition where I had to improvise something. If I hadn't got that little part I would never have had the *nerve* to go back. There's always a key moment, as a child or a teenager, when you get that bit of encouragement that gives you the guts to go on living. I went to class in the Dallas Theatre Centre, the only theatre Frank Lloyd Wright ever built, where they were doing Brecht and Ibsen, as well as musicals, comedies, a bit of everything. In *Stop the World, I Want To Get Off*, my sister and I played the two young girls, and your ex-husband, Tony Newley, was an idol of mine when I did his plays.'

'You were married once very young and you've never married again. Now you've been with your boyfriend for twelve years. Is it important for you to have a man in your life?' I asked.

'It used to be. I've gone through my life dating a lot of very interesting people and I used to think it was important to have a man *per se*. But if Mark and I broke up I don't even know who I'd date now.'

'Pickings are slim, aren't they?' I said.

'As you get older you realise the decent men who wanted to settle down and have a family did that – and they're still there,' Morgan said ruefully.

'And your perspective changes as you get older. You put up with a lot *less* than you would when you were younger. Been there, done that, don't want to do it again. Mark is a wonderful, honourable man and that's important to me, and *very* hard to find in this town. If for some reason we were to split up, I don't know if I'd even be interested in dating. If I had to put up with a lot of things I didn't like I'd rather be alone. I *love* the idea of one man and one woman for life, but unfortunately that doesn't always work out. I see so many friends who are unhappy and getting divorced. I'm also set in my ways, and older guys are too. I'm very independent. I don't want to be a slave or a toy to some guy. Many successful men think that if you're an actor, your career is just a toy and you're supposed to be able to walk away from it and go on vacation with them,' said Morgan.

'You use the word actor. Do you call yourself an actor or an actress?' I asked.

'I call myself an actor – that's the way I was brought up.'

We debated this for a while as I believe certain things have to have gender definitions, then I asked her what was the true secret of looking young.

'I believe it has to be based in science. Our cells are actually just great big chemistry labs and we are beginning to understand more about the way our bodies utilise what we put into them. I also take a holistic approach, like using detox teas. If I start to get bags under my

eyes, or shadows, I take detox stuff and drink detox teas, to get rid of them,' she explained.

'What is a detox tea?' I asked.

'Any health food store sells things that are detox,' she said. 'I take all the different teas. Some are diuretic and cleansing, some are supposed to get rid of cellulite if you take regularly, because cellulite is just bad storage of fat.'

'Do you feel that scientists are getting to the point where they really can start to conquer the ageing process?' I asked. 'We have made incredible strides in the last forty, fifty years.'

'I think we've made incredible strides in the last *five* years. As people are living longer, it's very encouraging that we'll be able to live longer, feeling better, looking better and less prone to the degenerative diseases that come with age.'

'Last week in the *New York Times* they wrote about the new osteoporosis drug and mentioned that one of the side-effects is that it helps prevent breast cancer,' said Morgan.

Katy Kass photographed Morgan, Sean Connery and me at my birthday bash, 23 May, 1998, in Hollywood.

'Do you really believe there are face creams and products in toners that can actually change the surface of the skin?' I enquired.

'Yes, the glycolic acid that we talked about earlier, Retin A, and there's this new Cellex-C which contains 5 per-cent vitamin C topically applied. Ageing is a break-down or deterioration of all those building processes in the cells. So skin is not as strong and firm as it used to be. The same process that causes you to get degenerative diseases as you get older, because your immune system is compromised, because it's not regenerating as it used to, is the process that makes you visually age too. So ideally we must halt or reverse these processes. They are getting closer – they're doing research on the human-geno project, tabulating every gene in the human body. Already they're identifying genes that cause hereditary diseases. They don't quite know how to fix them yet, but each step like this is a step in the right direction. When we're younger our cells tend to live longer and they reproduce more strongly. The longer we live, the more those cells reproduce, the more stressed out they get, from all the pollutants we put in our body, the wear and tear of age, too much sun and booze, too much of everything. The future generations, especially the next generation coming up, should have a lot of things available to them to keep them young and healthy a *lot* longer. They may not *look* better if they keep going in the sun, but they will have access to a lot of scientific discoveries that will prevent the things we all fear as we get older, like bones breaking. Wrinkles are just where the collagen is not reproducing.'

'Do you think that what we eat affects the way we look?' I asked.

'I think what we eat has a *lot* to do with it. I think Americans eat incredibly badly,' she agreed.

'I'm glad an American's admitted this,' I grinned.

'Americans eat too much and all the wrong things. Not only junk food, which we all know is bad, the fries, the hamburgers and all that, but even people who try to eat healthily don't necessarily pay as much attention as they should. I was talking to a friend who is trying to bring up her baby as a vegan. They're not even giving this poor baby milk! They're not giving it fruit or meat. The body's like a chemistry lab, so you *have* to furnish it with certain things that will build it properly. There are so many bad fad diets. They can publish anything, but that doesn't mean they will work.'

I congratulated Morgan on her scientific expertise then asked her what was the latest method of getting rid of wrinkles.

'There's a new peel that doctors can do all over your body. It's similar to a face peel although *not* as stringent, but glycolic acid also works, as should Retin A or any of the new retinols. Scientists are also working on products that are supposed to build collagen from the *inside.*'

'You are a mine of information,' I said admiringly.

'Well, I never stop learning,' she smiled.

Several days later Morgan came to my birthday party looking fabulous in a pink strapless dress, and not a day over 30. Her flawless skin shows the sensational results of a disciplined programme of proper scientific skincare, something from which we could *all* learn.

'The body's like a chemistry lab, so you have to furnish it with certain things that will build it properly.'

LOUISE FENNELL

THE JEWELLER'S GLAMOROUS WIFE

Louise Fennell has been a close friend since the mid-80s. Married to handsome jeweller Theo Fennell, they are amongst the most popular couples in London, and I know many men in London who fancy her madly. When we first met she was tall, mousy-blonde, attractive and slightly on the plump side, with an infant daughter Emerald. In the intervening years she has lost pounds, changed her hair to golden blonde, had another child Coco, who is my adored god-daughter, and has become a glamorous beauty. Louise holds regular sales of designer clothes and samples in her house and has often been compared looks-wise to Patsy in *Ab Fab*. I went to have tea with Louise on a fine June day at their charming house in Chelsea.

Louise was wearing a long brown suede skirt and a cream jumper, her blonde hair casually framing her chiselled face.

With her two wide-eyed daughters listening raptly, while pretending to do their homework, Louise and I chatted over tea and cake at her kitchen table.

Louise Macdonald was born in 1956 in South Wales and had an idyllic rural childhood with minimal schooling, leaving school at 16.

'I tried to be a secretary but simply couldn't spell so I spent most of my time on the telephone to my friends,' she laughed. 'My first job was for *The Economist* – when my boss came into my office one day wanting to ask me something, I was on the telephone to a friend and it didn't occur to me to get off. He waited and waited and eventually when I hung up he said "You're fired". So then I went to work for Thea Porter, which was heaven. She was an incredible designer in the 60s and 70s, and inspired me in every creative aspect of my life.'

'It was in Thea's Soho boutique that I first met you in 1977. I remember how young you looked and now, at 41, you're almost the youngest woman in my book,' I said. 'You look better than twelve years ago. You've become truly glamorous. You've done a wonderful make-over, and went on a diet which really worked. How *did* you lose almost a stone?'

'It was a kind of anti-diet really,' Louise answered. 'Having spent all my life on a diet it was quite the opposite of dieting. I actually ate three proper meals a day. This was revolutionary, because I never ate breakfast, often skipped lunch and then snacked all afternoon. The secret is not to eat *anything* in between. That can be difficult and some days you slip, but the principle is there. All Bran and fruit for breakfast, then for lunch and dinner it doesn't

matter. No booze, no white flour and *no* sugar, are the only rules.'

'Did stopping drinking make you lose weight too?' I asked.

'It certainly helped, because if you don't drink you won't lose your willpower so you're not tempted to eat things that you shouldn't. Also you don't have that hung-over tired feeling the next day which makes you want to scoff all sorts of unsuitable things.'

'I know you enjoy parties without drinking, now,' I said.

'Easily, and now I've got used to it, I'm much more confident. I have more energy and I remain relatively coherent while everybody else becomes *less* coherent as the evening goes on. And I like that – probably for some horrid smug reason!'

'And you can drive your husband home.'

'And I can drive him round the bend too! I do have a lovely time without drinking, which surprises me.'

'Actually you never drank a lot, unlike some people we knew,' I said. The girls giggled knowingly and Louise told them to get back to their homework.

'Your figure has improved tremendously by losing a stone,' I said.

'Yes, I suppose it has, but I never weigh myself and I don't worry about it anymore. I used to spend a lot of time worrying about my build and now I don't. So I probably do put on weight sometimes but then I lose it again. I just don't think it's that important. I do know as you get older it's important to be healthy, not fat nor too thin.'

'You've said you don't take any vitamins, but not even C in the winter?' I asked.

'No, because one vitamin C pill supposedly contains the equivalent of thirty oranges in one pill. I think if I was *designed* to eat thirty oranges I'd have been a monkey living in a tree, for goodness sake! I actually think they might

Photographed by Eddie Sanderson at Royal Ascot, 17 June 1998 – hence the OTT hats!

be dangerous. Obviously if a doctor says you need more iron I'm prepared to believe him, but on the whole I think if you eat enough fruit and vegetables there's absolutely no reason why you would *need* extra vitamins.'

'What about exercise?' I asked her.

'I never do any formal exercise routine. I just run around a lot and do fifty sit-ups every other day maybe. I don't play any sports because I think your bones and knees can't have been made for jumping about after a certain age,' she said emphatically.

'I agree, too much exercise is as bad as too little,' I said.

'Also, with two daughters under 13, I'm *constantly* running around.

'Now you're 41, Louise, which today is the equivalent of what 28 used to be. Forty is by no means old any more. It's not even properly middle-aged. There's a new generation of women between 40 and 70 who have achieved an *incredible* amount.'

'And I hope they will continue,' said Louise. 'I know I want to continue working.'

'In another ten years the girls will have fled the nest and Theo will still be making jewellery. What do you think *you* will be doing?' I asked.

'I will definitely always work. I've worked since I was 16. There are millions of things I still want to do, and not just for the sake of money. I'd like to produce television documentaries and definitely do more travelling,' she said decisively. 'I want to go back to India – there are so many places to see. I'd really like to do a bit of challenging, exploring travel too, rather than 5-star stuff.'

'You have lovely skin. What's your secret?' I asked.

'I don't know *how* I've got good skin, but if I have it's probably genetic,' she said generously. 'I just use ordinary Johnson's Baby Lotion to take my make-up off, I don't take my eye make-up off, it just comes off. I think too much rub-

bing is probably not good for your eyes and rubbing your eyelashes will make them fall out. Then Clinique moisturiser, some stuff called Clinique Exceptionally Smooth Cream which is an anti-itching cream and quite good if the skin's looking a bit blotchy. That's it, that's my beauty routine.'

I asked Louise if she was wearing make-up now and she said it was Clinique compressed powder foundation. 'If it's a big gala I do slap on plenty of stuff – I try to be quite exaggerated. I always wear lipstick because it makes me feel dressed.'

'So how do you de-stress?' I asked.

'I ask myself *why* I'm getting so worried about whatever it might be. If I can actively do anything to control the situation, then I'll do it; if I can't then I just accept that I'm wasting my time worrying about it,' she grinned.

'That's a really cool philosophy,' I said. 'Actually I've never seen you lose your temper or your cool. You've always been the epitome of calm, even when the two girls were running you ragged as babies.'

'I don't lose my temper, it's true,' she said. 'My father brought us up to believe that ranting and raving is very self-indulgent and horrible for everyone concerned. No matter *what* American psychologists say, I still agree with him. I have always tried to treat my family with love and respect and I'm happy to say they return the same in abundance.'

'Do you think that's in-built in you? Do you never lose sleep worrying about problems?'

'I do sometimes lose sleep – that's when I know I'm getting stressed – but basically stress is just thoughts going round and round your head. I reckon if it's come round more than three times I have to actually stop and tell myself I'm going a bit bonkers and then relax and go to sleep. My father is like that, he is just totally bomb-proof and he brought me up to be that way as well.'

'Basically do you consciously believe in the power of positive thinking, or do you just feel that you, Louise, have been lucky to have been given such positive values?'

'I think I believe in it consciously which *was* the way I was brought up… I can take self-control a little too far. I think it's important not to repress all your feelings too much, because you can become so cool that you miss the point. I want to enjoy all the moments of my life. I don't want to waste time worrying about too much unimportant stuff. So I've made a really conscious decision and I look into that a lot and read quite a bit.'

'Do you read books or manuals, like Buddhism or other alternatives that help give you positivity?' I asked.

'Yes, some spiritual things are fascinating. Although I'm not a very religious person there are so many philosophical questions to be answered. I don't think it's something I considered when I was young. As you get older you do suddenly wonder "What's the point? Where am I going? What am I doing?" Then as friends become ill or die you realise that life is too short, and you think therefore I really must get the best out of it and have a good time,' she said.

'Yes, life is just a long weekend,' I sighed. 'I'm glad you've already realised this, Louise, because most people don't until they're much older – I certainly didn't. The speed at which time passes is quite terrifying.'

'Yes, but I've learnt a lot from you, Joan, because you've always lived in the moment, and you're a great one for grabbing life and just going for it and letting the bad things go. It's very unusual, practically unique.'

'Thank you. I learnt that from a month long seminar in Arizona, called Sedona. They teach you a method of releasing all negative thoughts. And concentrating on the positive ones,' I said. I asked Louise who her heroines were.

'There are masses of incredibly heroic people in the world who aren't necessarily famous, so I think that the ordinary people in the street, the ones who are, to put it bluntly, wiping bottoms in madhouses, are my heroes. I admire the good, and they're often not the people who end up being *great*, because unfortunately the ones who *are* great tend to be more single-minded and selfish,' she said.

'If you were allowed one beauty product on a desert island, what would it be?'

'It would have to be Johnson's Baby Lotion. Useful, too, because if I was there for long enough, I'd be bound to have a baby and so I could use it for that too.'

'You have developed a wonderful, individual chic; people say, "Louise always looks great, she's so stylish." You always look as though you spend a hundred thousand pounds a year on your clothes.'

'Which certainly isn't true,' she laughed.

'So how did you develop your distinctive style?' I asked.

'I've always loved clothes since I was quite young,' she answered. 'I used to make things for myself out of old tie-dyed table-cloths and damask curtains and precarious bits of elastic.

'One vitamin C pill supposedly contains the equivalent of thirty oranges in one pill. I think if I was designed to eat thirty oranges I'd have been a monkey living in a tree.'

Everything would then be exposed at excruciating country dinner parties. Thea Porter taught me to love the exotic, she was such a brilliant designer... her clothes were incredibly rich, gypsy looking, wonderfully glittering – that Eastern stuff which I adore. I always loved dressing up as a child, playing around and making hats and just fiddling with bits and pieces. Every person has something beautiful about them and when you know what it is you must draw attention to it,' she continued. 'I've always wanted to look different to everyone else, so I choose things that are quite fun and slightly extrovert – but we're not talking clowns here; either very simple or a bit fluffy and feminine too. I avoid prints as a rule.'

'You were the first person I saw with a Lulu Guinness bag, three years ago,' I said.

'I love Lulu's bags, they're very feminine. And works of art in their own right.'

'You also wear a lot of tailored things like Ralph Lauren?' I queried.

'Yes, there's nothing better than a really good cut. Ralph Lauren's great because he designs for American women, who tend on the whole to be bigger, and as I'm nearly six foot, the French designers aren't any good because everything is too small, too short and doesn't fit.'

'Your wardrobe has just a few perfect things in it, true?' I asked.

'I have a *very* short rack with mostly new clothes because I get rid of everything else... usually I get rid of it within six months,' she said firmly.

'It's *amazing* how you can do that – I'm dreadful because I hang onto things. I always think "I may wear this again". It's an art to chuck out clothes, I envy you,' I said.

'I either re-sell things or give them away if they're good, or if they are worn out I throw them away.'

'Would you throw away that jolly nice suede skirt?'

'Yes, quite soon, because it's getting worn out,' she said.

'And you actually chuck it into the dustbin?' I asked.

'Yes,' she grinned, 'because it will be worn into the ground.'

I looked over at Emerald. 'Your daughter might like to have it.'

'No she won't, because she likes her own stuff. I always think that's a myth, keeping it for the children, because they hardly ever wear their mother's things. They'll have their own style.'

'So you never miss any of the clothes you've thrown out?' I asked.

'I've never ever missed a single thing because something new is always so much more fun and exciting.'

'I once chucked out my favourite pair of blue jeans, very tight, an almost washed out pale blue, but they fitted like a glove and I regretted it for *years*,' I said. 'I also gave away a few *Dynasty* dresses, then I saw them in auction houses going for about six thousand pounds.'

'Well, that's definitely different,' said Louise. 'Those are historical.'

'But good clothes aren't cheap,' I said. 'So if you buy an expensive Ralph Lauren suit, you'll only wear it for six months and then you'll chuck it?'

'Well no I won't. I'll wear it twice or three times and then I'll re-sell it... it's a waste for clothes to sit in cupboards. They might as well be worn until they're worn out, because if they're *really* beautiful things it's tragic that they're only going to be enjoyed by one person, they might as well go all over the place. I've always liked the idea of clothes having a life of their own, a history,' said Louise.

'You're going to visit me in Los Angeles and before that you're going to New York. You'll be away for ten days in all kinds of weather. What's your ideal wardrobe for a trip?'

'A black dinner jacket trouser suit, probably

Louise and Theo Fennell, photographed by Nils Jorgensen.

Ralph Lauren, various different vests and tops to go underneath. Then a couple of slip dresses... which are my favourite things at the moment. One is a sort of lacy embroidered thing with a satin slip underneath and then a kind of 'Voyage' type velvet trimmed cashmere cardigan over the top... It's very comfortable, which is also vital – I never have a good time in tight clothes. Then I'd take some white T-shirts and a suede dress. I'm really keen on suede at the moment. That's probably about it.'

'You wouldn't take blue jeans and black

jeans and black pants and beige trousers and fourteen different jackets, which is what I do?' I said ruefully. 'I *always* pack too much.'

'I might take a pair of black trousers but I wouldn't take jeans because I've got a fat bottom and I look terrible in them. I'm bad on shoes – I never have decent ones, because I can never see any that I like. So I use the excuse that if they're looking at my feet I've failed. I do have a few clothes rules like:

1. Don't ever try to look like someone else.

2. Never wear short skirts if you have bad legs or tight things over fat bits, i.e. basically always cover the parts you're unhappy with and display the good parts.

3. Stay away from prints/dots/stripes except in extraordinary circumstances. Scarves are the most useless things in the world. Unless you need to catch a horse or possibly fix a fan belt.'

'I have a great idea for you, Louise. You should start a service called "Organising your closet". You could look over women's wardrobes and chuck out everything that's not appropriate,' I said.

'It wouldn't work because the reason you keep something is because it's part of your history, it reminds you of the past and is almost like a diary in clothes. That's probably true for many people.'

'True. I was looking at a blue pinstripe suit which I only wore once and was saying "I must ditch this". But I wore that suit the day I won my court case with Random House. It had history so I decided I couldn't get rid of it,' I said. 'Now, hair – you've done wonders with yours.'

'*Hugh's* done wonders with my hair,' Louise answered. 'The magic Hugh Green. It's a good idea to put your hair up when you're over 40 – they say cutting it takes off years, but I think that putting it up has the same result but still allows you to have your hair down sometimes... I don't think short hair looks good on tall women and I need all the femi-

'Jewellery, feathers and a big smile, that's the trick.'

ninity I can get! I love my hairpieces. I'm mocked for them, but I don't care – I think they're brilliant. I've got one that's like a ponytail – if you've only got fifteen minutes to change you just shush your hair up, it's got a great sort of plait that hooks on over the top, it's terrific. It makes me look like a real girly girl and blokes like it. Lots of hair is very feminine and as I don't have tons of it why not add some? It's dressing up... I love dressing up, it's so much fun. Magazines write so excessively about exercise and diet and youth and pert bosoms and many of us have got confused and think we've got to be physically perfect. But I believe that life's too short for all that, and I also think that there are many ways of cheating a bit, and glamming up is just easier and more fun.

'I'm glad you like glamour... because I think that you are one of our most glamorous English women. When I look at some of the others in the glossies it's as though they're *ashamed* of being glamorous. Dowdy clothes and they have four wisps of hair which they back-comb to try and make it look good but it never does. It's much better to get a hairpiece or put a hat on,' I said.

'Anything sparkly by the face is always a good thing, isn't it? Jewellery, feathers and a big smile, that's the trick,' smiled Louise.

'Does Theo give you unlimited access to his jewels?' I asked.

'It is wonderful to be able to wear all Theo's jewellery and it also means I can have something to match anything which is fantastically lucky. I love being able to do that... People are so misled about beauty. Beauty *really* comes from the inside, so slap on some make-up and a good dress and the rest is down to the person's character. No amount of nipping and tucking and exercising is going to make somebody desirable if they have an undesirable character.'

'And so, Louise, in fifteen or twenty years will you still want to look glamorous? You look wonderful now but when people say, "she's 60, she's 70, she should give it up now" – you won't, will you?'

'Of *course* not. My grandmother was dressing up until she died at 76, and although my mother isn't like that she's just naturally beautiful because she's such a lovely person. She only needs to put lipstick on and she looks glamorous, but that's because she's always smiling. Smiling's better than a face-lift really.'

'And loving as well. You have a lot of love in your life, you have good friends, wonderful daughters and wonderful Theo,' I said.

'It is so important, to give love, then you get

a lot back. In our Western society we're all so driven, always feeling you *must* be better, *got* to get on, *got* to do more, *got* to be *cleverer*, prettier, richer, instead of saying actually you're doing your best, so give yourself a break and enjoy it,' said Louise. 'And so, I would say that my philosophy is to be compassionate to others and to myself, not so compassionate that I am a *slave* to everyone else, but just to be kind. I think that makes life much much easier. Oh, and don't think too much about how to fix everything or how to get your own way, just go with the swing and do your best. I'm a bit of a hippy, really,' she laughed.

'You're the most glamorous hippy I've ever seen. Do you think you get the face you deserve after a certain age?' I asked. 'Because I know many women over 40 who look dreadful, and they're usually people who don't think good thoughts.'

'Absolutely, without a *doubt* you get the face you deserve. Women can have big noses and wonky eyes and thin lips but at the end of the day they can still look absolutely lovely, if they are lovely *inside*. As long as you make a certain amount of effort then the rest *has* to come from inside. I believe envy and anger make people ugly inside and out. I'm whizzing through life so fast I don't have *time* to look back. Why drag all this clobber along with me? Why not just let it go when it's not of any use to me or anyone? I keep photographs to remind me of special things but sometimes we can collect so much stuff that it's quite stifling. All that bumpf to sort out. I think I could lose every material thing I have without shedding a tear – my husband, children, family and friends are what matter and all that I really care about.'

With that tea was over and I spent the rest of the afternoon playing with Coco. Louise Fennell seems to have her act totally together. A woman of taste and charm about whom we will be hearing much more in the years to come.

FEW WOMEN IN THEIR forties look younger than Fiona Fullerton. Her infectious giggle and totally toned dancer's body could belong to a twenty-something and it's hard to believe that this golden-haired 41-year-old has been in show business for over thirty years. Fiona is one of Britain's most well known and versatile actresses whose present career encompasses journalism, broadcasting and television presenting. Petite with amazing pale green eyes and short blonde hair, she also writes a series of articles on gardens and houses and is a shrewd property developer.

She was catapulted to international stardom at the age of 11, starring in a big screen musical version of *Alice's Adventures in Wonderland* alongside Peter Sellers, Ralph Richardson and Dudley Moore. Her starring roles in both theatre and television have gained outstanding critical acclaim, most notably as 'Paulina' in *Death and the Maiden*. Her 'astonishing dexterity' was hailed by the critics; as Eliza Doolittle in *Pygmalion*; and as Constance in Somerset Maugham's elegant comedy *The Constant Wife*.

Because she's so pretty it's easy to forget the diversity of Fiona's career. She's one of the few actresses who have starred in the West End

FIONA FULLERTON
WORKING MOTHER

Photographed by Eddie Sanderson in Fiona Fullerton's garden in Weybridge, 19 June 1998.

in both a straight play and a musical: opposite Keith Michell in *The Royal Baccarat Scandal* and playing Guinevere opposite Richard Harris in *Camelot*.

In the hugely successful TV series *The Charmer*, she played the manipulative society beauty, Clarice Manners, opposite Nigel Havers. She was a Bond girl, Russian spy Pola Ivanova, in *A View to Kill* and her leading men have ranged from Roger Moore and Richard Harris to Michael Crawford and Robbie Coltrane.

WE MET IN THE charming Georgian house in Weybridge, where Fiona, her second husband, businessman Neil Shakell, to whom she is happily married after a youthful divorce, and their two children live. The mature garden was in full June bloom with roses climb-

***The Bond Girl:* A View To A Kill, 1985.**

ing everywhere, as was Fiona's adorable red-headed toddler Lucy. We sat outside in her lush garden sipping tea while Fiona kept a watchful eye on her.

'You had your first baby in your late thirties – how did it affect you physically,?' I asked.

'Since having Lucy in 1995, my skin and body have changed enormously. I don't know if you found that when you had yours, because you were much younger, a lot of things tend to change when you have a baby later in life. However, I'm not really concerned because I've never been obsessional about how I look or my weight or body image. But the change in the texture, colour and pigment of my skin, and the fact that I tend to break out a lot more since Lucy was born, is quite extraordinary. I cover up my spots with brilliant cosmetics, like Max Factor's Creme Puff, which is a powder that covers like a foundation. I use Max Factor quite a lot. I started using their products when I was their international face; they are actually very good, particularly if you're doing photographs. Other things also change after pregnancy, like your hair, the shape of your body and even your feet. My feet went up a whole size after I had Lucy! I put on four stone when I was carrying her so my feet spread. It's horrible because I had thirty pairs of beautiful shoes that I can't wear now. Of course, I don't lead that sort of life anymore so I don't need them, which is fine. But the skin problem's not something I worry about.'

'Well your skin always looks beautiful, Fiona. It's rather translucent, so you must have taken good care of it all your life. Are you religious about taking off your make-up and using moisturiser?' I asked.

'I'm probably as careful about it as any woman, but we *all* have moments when we lapse otherwise we'd be completely self-obsessed saints. I'm a very lazy person – I don't even go to the gym,' she grinned.

'I am actually a homebody, and all I was looking for in my party period was the right person with whom I could share my life.'

'Running around after a two-year-old and an eight-year-old is enough exercise. Have you got a nanny?' I asked.

'Yes, but at night we look after them ourselves,' she said.

'What happens when you go out?'

'We don't want to go out,' she laughed. 'I used to be known as a raving party girl. It was fun to be out there in the bright lights but I never really enjoyed it. People are quick to label one in this business. I am actually a homebody, and all I was looking for in my party period was the right person with whom I could share my life. Both Neil and I are newly-weds and still very much in love, and I just *love* being at home with him and my babies. I've acquired not only lots of different careers but also interesting hobbies like gardening and I would rather spend my time doing those things,' she said.

'You're a journalist, a mother, a wife, an actress and a newly wed. That's a *hell* of a lot of things to balance, Fiona.'

'*And* a property manager and landlord,' she said, as little Lucy came up to give her another hug. 'For twenty years I've been interested in doing up properties. I've always been a bit of an interior designer, and I love anything to do with fabrics and texture, antiques and paintings. I've collected all my life and I spent a great deal of time and energy doing up every home that I had and getting it right.

'Then quite by accident I got into the letting market by renting out one of my homes and I realised how much money you could make from renting good properties, so over the years I invested in property in central London. I take a property that needs complete renovation, gut it and start again; I design it, and deal with all the plumbers and architects and carpenters myself. I enjoy it, although it's sometimes a nightmare, but now it's one of my main businesses and *very* lucrative.' She smiled as Lucy squeezed her in a bearhug and I asked her about diet dos and don'ts.

'I haven't eaten red meat since 1980 but I *do* eat fish and chicken occasionally. I won't eat anything with four legs. It's not for moral reasons, it's purely for my digestion. I used to get chronic migraines, then someone suggested that I try cutting out meat. When I stopped the difference was extraordinary. I've never had a headache since,' she said.

'Whenever I get indigestion it's usually because I've eaten a steak or some heavy meat dish, so I don't eat them very often, but occasionally I need a steak for energy,' I said.

'Meat is tough for any digestive system to cope with. It's different for blokes. Dietwise I try and eat sensibly but I *do* indulge. I'm not so obsessed that I won't ever eat chocolate or cakes or dessert and I love ice cream. I always use sweeteners because I like sugar and I drink, but mainly champagne or the odd glass of wine. Eating is such a pleasant pastime. I love Italian food so we eat a lot of pasta. I like carbohydrates and vegetables and you can eat enormous quantities of those and never get fat. It's the cream and the fat in food that piles on the pounds. You shouldn't do what Americans do, which is graze all the time, constant picking. I *never* eat between meals, I just eat sensibly during the day. When I was younger I only used to eat one big meal, which is bad, and I *never* ate breakfast. Now I realise, having children, that you can't do that. It's terribly important you have breakfast. Then a nice little lunch and a nice little supper. And a nice glass of wine.'

We laughed. 'You really are enjoying life, aren't you?' I said.

'*Absolutely*,' said Fiona. 'You see I'm married to a man who lost his wife seven years ago through cancer. She was only forty-two when she died and Neil nursed her for the last two years in this house, administering all the drugs and injections. When you've been through a life-changing experience like that many things cease to be important, so I have learnt vicariously through Neil how unimportant a lot of this shit is. All the little things that used to worry me in the past don't worry me at all. Neil is the most extraordinary, calm man, and he's the perfect match for me, because he lets me be volatile and emotional and let off steam but also keeps me calm. Absolutely nothing will ever worry him, because watching your wife die is the most terrible experience that any man could go through. My philosophy now is to adapt to the pace of life so that it suits *you*, so that you stop dancing to somebody else's tune. I was always doing things to please other people; I was *always* trying to be something that I wasn't. The image that people had of me was not me at all. Now I've learned to be true to myself and do the things that appeal to me, to do it at my own pace and not get upset about

things. For example, we all get upset when we're driving. Road rage at people cutting across...'

Right on cue a helicopter flew noisily overhead.

'I used to get into such a flap if I was going to be late,' Fiona continued. 'Now I think life's too short to worry about that,' she said.

'There's a saying I'm starting to live by – will any of this matter in a year's time?' I said.

'I have several friends right now who have cancer. One gets terribly upset about it, but then one says, there's nothing I can do about it except be as supportive as possible. I do think there's a lot more cancer around now, more than ever, and I think a lot may be brought on by –'

'The stress of life? Or by the crap we eat – everything's covered in pesticides today. Are you careful with your children?' I asked.

'Our kids love fruit and vegetables, particularly broccoli, which thrills me because it's so beneficial but most children hate it. And of course we *never* allow fizzy drinks.'

'Thank goodness, they're pure poison. Do you take vitamins?' I said.

'I've just started taking vitamin E because of my skin.'

I asked her if she had heroines.

'I became an actress by accident. Originally I wanted to be a ballet dancer, and my heroine was Margot Fonteyn, so I started ballet at three, and became quite a conscientious, serious little ballet dancer. I've always been a huge admirer of Katherine Hepburn who was quite extraordinary for her time because she really fought against the Hollywood system. She developed a style of her own that was unlike any other screen goddess. I loved the fact that she made wearing trousers acceptable. She was the epitome of casual chic, which is something that I absolutely adore, and she loathed dressing up which I do too.'

When I asked Fiona what single beauty product she'd take on a desert island she said:

'Concealer. During the day the one thing that I put on is a little bit of concealer under my eyes to hide the shadows round my nose and on my chin, that's all.'

'You've got really strong eyebrows, which are great. Do you do anything to those?'

'I put a touch of colour on them, not much'.

'You look like you have great hair, is it thick?'

'No, but there's a lot of it, so I keep it short because it's so fine. When I try to grow it, it just becomes fly-away,' she said.

I followed Fiona into the big country kitchen as she made some more tea and asked her how important love was to her?

'Very important,' she said vehemently. 'I always thought that I would marry again for love which is why I was on my own for so long – fourteen years before Neil. Of course there were boyfriends, but I never felt ready to settle down. The extraordinary thing is that as soon as I met Neil, that evening in 1994, in a restaurant, I knew immediately that I was going to spend the rest of my life with him. I rang my mother and said, "I think I'm going to marry Neil." And she said, "Are you sure?" He'd been a family friend for twenty years so we used

'I was constantly falling in love with totally unsuitable men who made me unhappy.'

to meet at weddings and various family events. It was when we were both unattached and we chatted that I knew immediately. I'm a great believer in love at first sight really.'

'Although you'd met him lots of times before,' I said.

'Sometimes it's that connection that you make with somebody as soon as you sit down and talk to them, something happens... it's not a physical thing, it's not a sexual thing, it's a real meeting of minds and of souls. It's about understanding each other, and wanting the *same* things together. He has the same values and the same outlook. Neil's also helped me to change my career and re-market my image. I'm now presenting my own television series called *Fiona Fullerton's Style Guide*. It's something that I've been keen to get into and I can't believe it's suddenly really happening.'

I asked her if she missed acting: 'I've turned down fifteen plays in two years because I just want to be with my baby... it's hard, because before marrying Neil I was playing some very good roles in the theatre.'

'I know, you got some wonderful reviews,' I said.

'Yes, I was even having meetings at the National but then of course I got pregnant so everything changed. But I don't regret it for *one* moment. I'm happier now than I've ever been and that's the only thing that's important in life. I truly believe that our physical looks come down to what's going on *inside*. If your soul is calm and you feel good then *that's* what keeps you looking great,' she said. 'I have *much* more confidence now in my forties than I ever had before. I was always slightly overawed by people, and very nervous in situations and I always felt insecure. Now I feel that I can do *anything*, which is why I've started branching out in different areas. A lot of that comes with the love of a good man, but I must qualify that by saying you *cannot* depend on a man to give

you these things, you *have* to find them first *yourself*,' she said. 'Then when you are complete, when you feel whole, then you meet the right man, and he fits into that jigsaw; you can flourish together. I always used to feel that a man would make me happy but I was constantly falling in love with *totally* unsuitable men who made me unhappy. But now that I feel so much better about myself Neil is the missing part of the jigsaw. I don't necessarily have everything, because there are so many more things that I *want* to achieve.'

I then asked Fiona how she felt about getting older.

'The older I get the more energy I have.' She swung Lucy up into the air and the little girl giggled joyfully. 'During my twenties when I wasn't working, I was always just wafting, having a good time, going out for lunch. Now every *moment* has to be grabbed and lived to the full and I'm busy, busy, *all* the time. The more you do the more you *want* to do. The children and I get up at the crack of dawn with the sparrows which I never used to before. It's another gorgeous day, and I'm up and running. I love that feeling of achieving something and then sitting down at the end of the day with Neil and a glass of wine and talking about all the exciting things that have happened. I feel sad about all those years I wasted in my twenties and thirties when I really wasn't achieving much.'

'You've achieved incredible harmony now. You have two children and all these different careers, a flourishing wonderful house and a wonderful husband, you've got it all Fiona.'

'I think I have,' she grinned.

I've always believed that houses and gardens give off vibrations and when we drove off I said to Judy, my assistant, 'their house has such good vibes and that comes from the happiness of the people who live in it.'

JERRY HALL

MODEL
EARTH-MOM

Thierry Mugler show, 1998.

IT WOULD BE EASY to dismiss Jerry Hall as just another glamorous supermodel and long-term consort of Mick Jagger. But there's far more to this gorgeous leggy Texan than meets the eye.

In 1977 I was celebrating the Queen's Silver Jubilee at my house in Los Angeles with my family and what was then known as the Brit-Pack. Rod Stewart, Samantha Eggar, Juliet Mills, Jane Seymour, Leslie Bricusse and many other dyed-in-the-wool patriots gathered around our outdoor barbecue, where Mayfair super-tailor Doug Hayward fried up British bangers instead of the traditional hot-dogs, and I ladled out the baked beans. Bryan Ferry had slipped quietly in while we were cooking with a tall blonde on his arm. My 13-year-old daughter Tara dashed out and whispered to me, 'Mummy, the most beautiful girl I've ever seen is inside with Bryan Ferry.'

I went to greet them and saw that Tara was right. Twenty-one-year-old Jerry Faye Hall was absolutely ravishing. Endlessly long wavy golden hair, endlessly long golden tanned legs in very short shorts, and big blue eyes with a guileless gaze.

She was utterly charming, sweet and, like most Texans, incredibly polite. I liked her

Photographed with Gabriel Jagger by Richard Young at Jerry Hall's home in Richmond, Surrey, 1 July 1998.

immediately and had no doubt she would continue her rise to modelling stardom. She had already been in the Yves St Laurent Opium perfume and Charles of the Ritz make-up advertisements, and the children had seen her on MTV in Bryan Ferry's video.

Since then Jerry has made a dozen films and in between having four children has not only continued a dazzling modelling career but become part of the English social scene. She also wrote an amusing anecdotal autobiography called *Tall Tales* and in 1987 her genuine comedy talent truly impressed me, when she played Cherie in *Bus Stop*, a role made famous by

Marilyn Monroe and to which she more than did justice.

Our paths have crossed many times over the years and her warmth and sweet Southern drawl have made each encounter delightful.

WE LUNCHED ON A beautiful June day in her late nineteenth-century mansion in the heart of Richmond. A large, comfortably furnished, extremely child-friendly house, it has stone floors, interesting pictures on the walls and a vast family-oriented kitchen. There's a strong feeling of peace and harmony, a lovely garden and a seemingly endless succession of rooms. A large Andy Warhol picture of Jerry dominates the dining room.

Adorable baby Gabriel, aged 8 months, cooed happily in a Moses basket on the floor of the large but cosy living room. Jerry looked glowing and exceedingly contented for a 42-year-old who'd recently given birth to her fourth child. She is incredibly funny and down to earth in the most charming Southern belle way, with a gorgeous figure. I couldn't resist asking her how she got back in shape so quickly.

'Breast-feeding,' she drawled. 'I'm still feeding Gabriel... I fed the other kids for four months but Gabriel won't take a bottle!' She shrugged happily. 'I'll do it for another year. We both like it. When I go out he screams for three hours; so he's got me.' She hugged the gurgling baby happily.

I told her what a fabulous disposition Gabriel had.

'He is a happy boy. He sleeps with me every night and goes with me everywhere. If I go to dinner, he goes. It's the new way of raising babies, very hippyish. I never did that with the other ones. I was strict – they were in bed by six o'clock and they had nannies, but I'm more relaxed now.'

I told her I'd seen lots of photographs of her and Gabriel at parties.

'Oh, he *loves* parties,' and she tickled Gabriel's plump feet. I asked how she exercised.

'I like swimming. And carrying Gabriel is like weight lifting. And of course sex,' she giggled.

'What about when you're pregnant?' I asked.

'I eat and drink *all* the time when I'm pregnant so I always gain a *huge* amount of weight. I eat an awful lot, sleep all the time and get very fat, but it goes quickly. I hold a lot of fluid, I take my rings off 'cos I just swell up. I always gain about 60 pounds.'

'So you've had four babies, each time you've gained around 60 pounds and you have this flat as a board stomach, which any 20-year-old would kill for,' I said admiringly.

'I've *always* had a very flat stomach.'

'How dare you!' I exclaimed. 'It's outrageous. What's the secret?'

'I swim quite a lot. And I do stomach exercises. Before I was pregnant, I'd do seventy sit-ups three times a week...' I touched her excellently toned stomach and she said, 'I have very good muscle tone. It's hereditary.'

'I can see those muscles. It's hard to believe you'd had *any* children.'

'I still wear a bikini. I *love* bikinis.'

I told her that I was fascinated by the miniature picture that Lucian Freud painted of her when she was pregnant.

'That just took a few weeks to paint. It was easy posing. I bought it for Mick but it's at an exhibition at the Tate Gallery now.'

We went into the dining room for a delicious organic lunch of poached salmon and rocket salad. I asked Jerry if everything she ate was organic, and she said:

'I get a lot of food from Planet Organic, that health food store in Notting Hill. It only sells organic food, and the most wonderful beauty products. Have you used Doctor Hauschka's natural products? His rose cream is superb. And I use Guerlain 12M cream as well. It's the best cream in the world. You put it on in the morning and at night and it gives you a simply wonderful glow. You wake up in the morning and look in the mirror and you go "I'm hooked!"' Jerry laughs, as she does a lot. Life seems to agree with her.

'So you're completely organic and you and the baby are thriving on it. What's your daily beauty routine?'

Batman, *1989.*

'I eat and drink all the time when I'm pregnant so I always gain a huge amount of weight.'

'Rene Guinot make-up remover, and Quickies mascara removal pads because they're oily and I don't like astringenty ones. I wash my face with Rene Guinot soap then I use very mild rose-water tonic and then my fantastic Guerlain 12M face cream. I don't wear much make-up. I am wearing Mac foundation today, but it's very light.'

I asked her if she thought make-up was a great protector from the elements and the sun.

'I certainly do. In the city with all the pollution it's a great barrier, but I really like wearing no make-up as often as possible at home. Although I love to wear make-up when I go out at night.'

I told her she'd looked like a gorgeous mermaid in her last Thierry Mugler Angel perfume advertisement and Jerry told me she was looking forward to doing another fashion show for him.

'You look fantastic when you're in flamboyant clothes, but you only seem to wear them in fashion shows. You actually always wear quite conservative clothes, Jerry. So what is your idea of style?'

'Classic clothes, good material, I like expensive clothes. I like sweater sets and kind of longish fitted skirts, because being tall and slim they look good. I don't really wear short skirts.'

'You've always worn chic, stylish clothes. You've never gone in for that tight mini-skirted look,' I said.

'Mini skirts are great but I think they look really stupid on women when they get older,' she said.

'But you're hardly old,' I laughed.

'I know but after the late thirties or early forties you shouldn't wear short mini skirts.'

'Mutton dressed as lamb,' I said. 'But still, wouldn't you agree that the whole attitude towards ageing and towards women has changed from our mothers' and grandmothers' time?'

'People are living so much longer now than they used to, so it makes middle age stretch out more. We're so much more aware of how important health is,' said Jerry.

She seemed so calm, even when Gabriel needed attention, that I asked her how she would de-stress.

'I get stressed if there's too much going on so I have regular massages. I love soaking in Dead Sea Salt and I also go to this back doctor who pops your back and neck, which is *brilliant* for stress. I also adore going for walks along the river, I find it very soothing.'

I told her that she was the supreme example of glowing motherhood over 40 and Jerry said that it was no longer considered unusual to have a baby at that age.

'I know *lots* of women who are getting pregnant in their forties,' she said. 'I used to think, God, I'm going to this party, I've got to rush – but with Gabriel I don't mind missing parties and staying home. I occasionally go to an event if I can bring him, but I don't feel that I'm missing anything. I've done it all,' she said. 'And Gabriel's obviously thriving on it, he's a real party animal. He loves people.'

'You're basically a working mother with a social life, a busy professional life and four children. How *do* you cope?'

'You must be very organised. And you can't do everything, you must delegate. Of course there are lots of things I'd like to do, but can't manage to fit in. I'm sure it's the same with you. It's impossible to do everything. I also make sure I take lots of vitamins. I get them from a natural doctor called Jack Temple, who supplies elements that are missing from our food because of over-farming, like calcium, selenium and zinc. He makes up a course of special vitamins for me. I've taken them for a year and I feel great. You can get them by mail and I do think they work, even my eyesight's improved,' she beamed.

The baby, who had now joined us for lunch and whom Jerry was breast-feeding, seemed so contented and jolly that whatever Jerry was doing was obviously working really well.

'Now my children are grown, I find I have so *much* energy to pour into other projects,' I said.

'I'm hoping I'll feel like you and be able to go back to work when I've got more time,' said Jerry.

'Of course you will. But you *must* appreciate your time with your children right now, because it goes so fast. I was looking at Sacha thinking, thirty-odd years ago he was my little baby, and now here's this great guy who's been escorting me to a round of parties. You'll be doing that with Gabriel in twenty years.'

'I hope so,' she laughed.

I asked her about diet.

'I watch what I eat *real* carefully. Mostly I have grilled fish or chicken and salad or vegetables and I stay away from potatoes, bread and cheese. Occasionally I have some of that 70 per cent cocoa chocolate from the Chocolate Society. I think a bit of chocolate every now and then is good for you,' she smiled.

'What about a little bit of wine?' I asked.

'I like to have a taste of wine but not much, but I wouldn't *dream* of drinking fizzy diet drinks. They are full of chemicals, and because I'm breast feeding, I don't want it getting to the baby.'

We both looked at Gabriel nursing contentedly and I asked her what she'd take on a desert island. 'Guerlain M cream,' she laughed, "cos I could use that *everywhere!*'

'Everybody envies your hair, Jerry. It's so beautiful, it must take *forever* to dry. Do you blow dry, or roller?' I asked.

'*Never* blow dry hair, that's *really* bad for it. I just towel dry it, and I only wash it once a week, because I like the oil. And if you leave your hair dirty after a while it stops becoming

'Never blow-dry hair, that's really bad for it. I just towel dry it, and I only wash it once a week.'

dirtier. It goes through a really dirty phase but then it stops producing so much oil and you don't have to wash it so often. I use mink oil on my hair. I get it in France and I put it on my hair as a conditioner.'

'You don't have any split ends,' I said.

'I use Mason Pearson hairbrushes and I'd *never* use a nylon comb or brush. I colour it

myself. I've used this French colour, Eugenie, for years. I took it to my natural healer, who's dowsed it and said that it's all right. He dowses all my beauty products and tells me whether they're bad or good. I took my mother, who's 74, to see him. He gave her just *one* treatment for the veins on her legs. They all went away,' she said triumphantly.

'If something is awful, think how to make it better and never feel defeated and give up.'

'So basically, you believe in purity in *every-thing* that you eat, drink, or put on your body?' I asked.

'Absolutely. I *never* wear nylon. It's really bad for you. I only wear silk tights from Christian Dior.'

I asked Jerry why she thought that nylon was so bad and she answered, 'My healer told me that your body absorbs the toxins and it stops your natural healing power. I wear cotton or silk, all natural fibres, as much as possible. Certain fibres that you *think* are synthetic, are actually natural fibres, like rayon, which is made of wood. Rayon's okay and so's polyester.'

'I hate polyester,' I said.

'I know, but nylon is *deadly*,' she said.

'What about bras? They're nearly all made of nylon,' I asked.

'I know, so I just wear silk or cotton from La Perla, who do lovely bras. That's my thing, Joan, I've gone completely natural.'

She looked at the contented sleeping infant in her arms and smiled beatifically.

'Aluminium, is also terrible, so you have to be careful that your hair colouring and deodorant doesn't have aluminium in it. They say aluminium causes Alzheimer's. You should also be careful with what sort of cooking pots you use. Maybe I sound a bit paranoid, but everyone I know is becoming incredibly careful of products which can be harmful, because we're already subjected to so many pollutants and toxins in the air.'

Jerry didn't hesitate in admitting that her heroine is Elizabeth Taylor and, perhaps like her, Jerry's basic philosophy is looking on the bright side, whatever is happening in her life.

'I think the main thing is having a positive approach to life, doing things that you want to do, and being happy about what you're doing. If something is awful, think how to make it better and *never* feel defeated and give up, because thinking positively can eventually turn things around,' she said.

'You always look so happy and you have incredible optimism. Do you ever lose your temper?' I asked.

'Sometimes I lose my temper but I apologise to people afterwards, and they say they hadn't realised I'd lost it, so obviously it's not *that* bad.'

'You must have had a fabulous childhood.'

'No,' she laughed. 'I had a pretty bad childhood. My mother was a very good mother and very positive, but my father wasn't there very often. He was one of those really macho guys who would drink and gamble and beat everyone up. I was the youngest so I didn't get beat up as bad as the others, but we all left home the minute we could, and I went to New York and started modelling at 16'.

The time had come for photographs, Gabriel cooing happily all the while. Jerry walked me out into the beautiful garden in the pale summer sunshine, the picture of elegant young motherhood in beige silk pants, cashmere sweater and pearls. We waved goodbye with promises to meet in France.

Two weeks later, true to her word, Jerry brought Gabriel to Ivana Trump's yacht in St Tropez to a party Ivana was throwing for me.

There was no question that Gabriel Jagger was the hit of the evening. And since his mother has been wowing everyone for years, it's fascinating to imagine what a hit *he's* going to be in 20 years time.

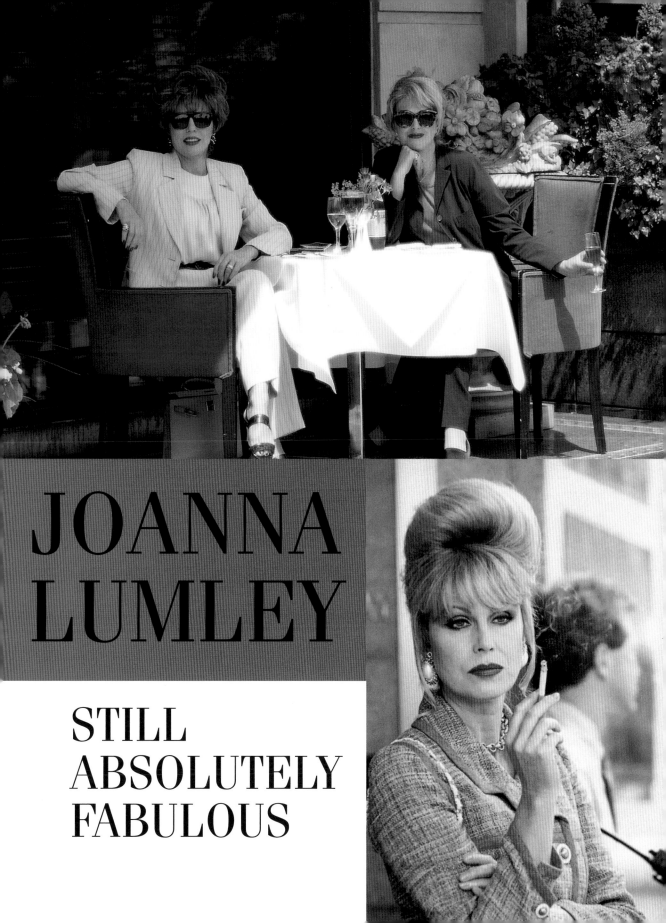

JOANNA LUMLEY

STILL
ABSOLUTELY
FABULOUS

Nobody epitomises over-50 is fabulous more than Joanna Lumley. Tall and deliciously blonde, her aristocratic mien defies her warm charm and droll humour. Intelligent, stylish *and* extremely approachable, Joanna is so popular that, next to the late Princess Diana, she is the wax figure at Madame Tussaud's most touched by the public. Forever remembered and beloved as Patsy in *Absolutely Fabulous*, Joanna Lumley has an impressive list of acting credits behind her.

Born in India in 1946, Joanna was convent-educated and arrived in London in the 60s, where she became a model and then an actress. She appeared in a number of films, including two *Pink Panthers*, and shot to fame as the karate-chopping but demure Purdey in *The New Avengers*. I first met Joanna in the late 60s with her then husband, comedy writer/actor Jeremy Lloyd, and they came to many parties at our house in London.

Joanna Lumley is enorm good-looking woman who doe too seriously, in spite of her cer

WE MET FOR LUNCH in the rest Athenaeum Hotel on a beautifu, june day. I knew Joanna would be punctual. Her taxi drew up in front of mine at *exactly* 12.29.

She looked stunning in a sleek brown trouser suit. We both ordered Kir Royales and endearingly, she asked me if I minded her smoking. I told her no but mentioned that few of the friends I'd interviewed smoked.

'I'm giving it up so I vary between none and ten. But in the evening when I'm with smokers I can virtually do a packet. I know *why* so many young women smoke today, because cigarettes are supposed to suppress your appetite,' she sighed. 'In France for breakfast they have a cup of black coffee and a cigarette, and all the young thin dancers and models smoke, to keep their weight down. I'm not a tremendous pro-smoking person,' she explained, 'but I can't see it as the biggest enemy, either. I don't think it's that much worse than drinking too much alcohol, or breathing in fumes from cars.'

'I agree with you about car fumes and pesticides that they spray onto vegetables,' I said.

'You can't find out whether it's there... all those secret things.' She shuddered. 'And now that so many animals are being fattened up on hormones, it's all going into our food. I've been a vegetarian for a long time. It was probably because I love animals, but then I discovered that you really *can't* feel fine about them being killed. I'm not proselytising. I don't want to try to convert people, but I just feel much better and more alert after food which I can graze on – I'm quite a grazer. I like to think about how

Photographed by Eddie Sanderson at the Athenaeum Hotel, London, 19 June 1998.

we might have eaten before this century's feasts, because we're so used to tucking into *rafts* of food these days. They could never have had this much before. In poorer countries they eat a healthier diet, based on bread or rice or polenta or spaghetti. The base is something humble, and then a little bit of fish, some meat and some protein is added on top.'

'Do you never eat chicken or eggs?' I asked.

'I do eat eggs, I'm not a vegan. I don't think there's anything wrong with that. We've always eaten animals, birds and fishes, but in a *much* more limited way. When the Bible said to kill the fatted calf, that was it. A *tremendous* celebration, so they ate some meat. We shouldn't eat it three times a day, though, or even three times a week. Moderation, Joan. It's the lesson in everything, isn't it?' said Joanna.

'Absolutely, even exercise. Do you exercise regularly?' I asked her.

'No, I don't actually. But I try to keep supple. I live in a tall house so I always run upstairs two at a time, many times a day. I try to keep fairly active and fit. And I think we *know* when we're getting a bit fat. You think "I've got to do some sit-ups". I can't do anything regularly, every day – apart from clean my teeth. People say "oh exercising only takes twenty minutes a day" and I reply "I could do three different tasks in twenty minutes. Seven phone calls, four letters, skim-read a script." Think sensibly. If you've got to get a saucepan out of a bottom shelf, get down and squat, lean forward and stretch,' she said.

'I believe people can exercise *too* much. It's now been proven that athletes and exercise gurus in their 40s and 50s who've been working out for twenty years have got aches and pains, arthritis and arthritic joints and hips now, all from over-exercising,' I said.

We ordered a simple lunch of soup and salad. 'How do you think women's bodies have changed in the last twenty years?' I asked.

'Maybe no one wants those curvy bodies anymore. All our clothes are big, baggy clothes. And all these boys' legs on women's bodies. Sophia Loren had a tiny waist and big bosom and hips; she looked like a woman and everyone *adored* her. But now people all look the same. The only way to get boy-thin is to starve yourself, and that's what all these young girls are doing, relentlessly dieting and exercising and trying to burn it off,' she said.

'It's also a fact that you and I and *many* women I've talked to have adapted their bodies. Women who were in their prime in the 50s or 60s, have now adapted their body shape into that of the 90s woman: not much of a waist or hips, skinny legs and as small a bosom as possible,' I said.

'Yes it's amazing how bodies change. If you look at newsreels of beauty queens of the 50s they had short, chubby little legs and huge thighs. Even the great glamour girls of the 40s like Betty Grable who was considered to have such amazing pins that they were insured for a million dollars, had dumpy legs by today's standards,' she said.

I asked Joanna how she started her career.

'I began photographic modelling at 18 and did it for three years before I got into the movies. I did a number of films, then television and stage. I never learned a thing from anybody, I just learned it all on the hoof, Joan, picking it up as I went along. I tried for RADA but was turned down when I was sixteen, and I didn't try again. I was too afraid that if they rejected me again, I'd have to give it up. RADA was going through a phase of hating 'posh' accents in those days and I'd got this voice, but I didn't know how to change it. It was absolutely the opposite of regional and if you didn't have a regional accent, you were nothing,' she said.

'Although you always look wonderful you're obviously not looks obsessed,' I said.

'I'm tall, Joan, and I've got broad shoulders which hides a *multitude* of sins. Shoulder pads are *marvellous* because they make clothes hang beautifully, so if you've got sloping shoulders or small shoulders it stops the rest of the body going outwards. They knew that in the 40s. You look razor slim if you have biggish shoulders,' she said.

'People have knocked the 80s clothes and shoulder pads but I *love* that look. Not everyone can wear the droopy cardigan look, and frankly it looks terrible on some.'

'Cardies *only* look good on the over 60s or under 30s,' joked Joanna.

'What do you like to wear?' I asked.

'In the 70s I adored the gypsy look with its frills and flounces, but when I look at photographs from then there was far too much going on. But I do think in the past clothes helped women to look beautiful. Victorian clothes, for example, made the most of your neck and bosom, and it didn't matter about your bottom and legs because they were hidden. And there were lovely lacey bits and pieces and darling little satin shoes, all very elegant things. It was easier to look prettier in "olden days" kind of clothes,' she said.

'The word "pretty" is almost anathema today,' I sighed. 'On the whole women don't want to look pretty. They look so androgynous that sometimes, in the street, I can't tell the difference between a boy or girl.' We laughed and I asked about her beauty regime.

'I wash my face with a gentle soap in the

'I've got broad shoulders which hides a multitude of sins. Shoulder pads are marvellous because they make clothes hang beautifully. They knew that in the 40s.'

Photographed by Richard Young at a London party, summer 1997.

evening, then put on Astral, which is rather like Nivea. And that's it. I put on my own make-up because, having been a model, I know how. And if I'm doing a film I usually understand the character well enough to know *how* she would do her face. I did Patsy, because I knew how Patsy would put it on: quite meticulously to begin with, but then once she'd had a bit too much to drink it would slip around a bit. When I was on tour with *Private Lives* I was using my own hair and it had a thirties sort of look. I was in Newcastle, and I went into a hairdressers and said "Just do my hair – either crimp it or marcel wave it, or put small rollers in." And they said, "We haven't got any rollers in the whole salon." I said "Well how would you do it?" and they said, "We'd just blow-dry it." I said, "No. You're hair*dressers*, you're supposed to dress hair, so can you? If you haven't got any-body older here who can remember, I can show you how it's done." They couldn't do it, they hadn't learned the skills of how to set hair properly.'

'Most hairdressers can *only* do today's style, cut and blow dry,' I said. 'Isn't that terrible? Where will they be if fashions change, which they always do?' I then asked Joanna if she thought make-up protected the skin.

'I think it does. A lovely old make-up man told me the best cover you can use is layers of Panstick, which will also clear up spots. I was aghast, because people tell you, "if you leave make-up on it'll wreck your skin", so I *always* clean my face at night. I don't mind wearing make-up and I never think, "I've got to get this filth off". Some people go on holiday and say

> *'I don't mind wearing make-up and I never think, "I've got to get this filth off." '*

'I'm going to have a scrubbed face', and they come back with a raft of spots, wondering what's happened,' she said.

'Do you protect your face from the sun?'

'If I lived in the South of France, I'd turn into an old turtle. But I don't like lying in the sun, so I would wear sunscreen and a hat,' she said.

I asked her how she de-stressed.

'If it's a stressy stress day sit down with whatever you like, a cup of coffee or the newspaper, or do a crossword puzzle for three minutes. Little rewards during the day stop stress building up,' she said.

I asked her if she had long hours on *Absolutely Fabulous.*

'No, but in the middle of the day, instead of food I require sleep, so I'd eat a piece of fruit, then find somewhere quiet where I could lie flat and sleep for 20 minutes, so I'd feel empowered again. Going straight to sleep is an art. You lie still and straight, like a resting vampire in your coffin and you calm right down. Put something light over you so you're covered, keep completely still and you'll drift off. I also think catnaps are invaluable. When I met President Clinton recently at Downing Street, I asked, "How *do* you manage this, on full power all the time?" and he said, "When I have to go from banquet to banquet, to speech to speech, to meetings, and travelling to and fro, I eat virtually nothing." I think his energy comes from not eating. If you eat, you usually feel tired afterwards – the snooze after lunch, the nap, that sort of thing. If you eat a *little* bit, a banana, a bite of an apple, something small, you keep going.'

I then asked Joanna how much sleep she needs.

'I got to bed at 2.30 this morning and was up at 8.30. But that's okay because I believe six hours is supposed to be the optimum amount of sleep. Much more than that is said to make you slow and sluggish. They conducted tests on

As *Purdey in* The New Avengers.

'Little rewards during the day stop stress building up.'

some people who insisted they needed eight hours, sleep. Scientists made them sleep only six hours a night for a month then report back. All of them said that they *felt* better and did their jobs better.'

'I saw *Girl Friday*, your desert island programme, which was great and *so* brave. What one beauty product would you take with you if you ever went back?'

'On that island I had *nothing*. No comb, no toothbrush, nothing. I would take a small tin of Vaseline. It can be lip gloss, it can do your nails if they're cracked, it can be face protection, if you're hurt it can be used as an antiseptic and, if you're trekking, it keeps your boots soft. So Vaseline is a goodie.'

'Your hair looked great in the programme, though,' I said.

'No, my hair's rotten, and it's very dyed. I've coloured it since I left school. It's full of wax today, but on the island sea water made it perfect. Magazines say rinse that salt out of your hair but I say leave that salt *in* your hair. It makes it soft, bouncy, and in perfect condition. And not rinsing the salt off my skin because it protected me. I went copper brown *without* moisturiser.'

'Well, you looked amazing at the end of it. I thought it was the most courageous thing I've ever seen,' I said.

'I was barking mad at the end because I'd only eaten a handful of rice every day for nine days. I was virtually starving, and only drinking water. It was so hot and sweaty that your mind was somewhere else. One thing I *always* take when I go away is a pareo – it's perfect. It's like a long sarong and you can tie it on your head if your hair's gone wrong, put it over your shoulders to stop yourself from burning, make it into a skirt if you want to be modest. It's one of the great all-purpose garments,' she said.

'I love pareos – I've got dozens,' I said.

'And I'd take some mascara. I like to make my eyes up,' she said.

'Women today don't do much to their eyes. Those 16-year-olds on magazine covers, with red lips and *no* eyes, look like rats.'

'I agree. One has to *balance* the face. You can wear masses up here' – she indicated her eyes – 'if you wear masses on here.'

I asked Joanna about her heroines and she said she loved people who travel. 'I love Dame Freya Stark, and all those pioneer travelling women.'

The charming actor Rutger Hauer – whom we both found rather fanciable, sauntered over to say hello and to invite us to have a drink with him and his wife. We joined them for coffee and after they left, we continued talking in the bar. I asked Joanna what her philosophy of life was.

'Don't think too far ahead. Give thanks every day for what you've got and be as nice as you can to people.'

'You're such a positive person. Do you believe that the power of positivity really benefits our lives?' I asked.

'Yes, I do. I think that you must *try*. You have to *try* to be nice, *try* to be positive, *try* to make a go of things. *Try* to make the party a good one, *try* to say thank you for everything you've got and be grateful to people. Don't just sit back and *expect* things to happen. John Lennon said in one of his songs: "The love you get is equal to the love you give". It's always a two-way thing,' she said.

'It's like that saying: "Isn't it amazing how lucky hard-working people are?"' I said and we *laughed*.

Later, as Eddie took pictures on the Athenaeum terrace on Piccadilly, we were highly amused by the amount of passers-by who stopped to gawp at us in amazement.

'Ooo'd've thought it,' said one old man staring open-mouthed. 'Patsy and Alexis 'avin' a drink togevver in the middle of London. Whatever next?'

Love Story, *1970.*

ALI MACGRAW
LITTLE ALI, HAPPY AT LAST

IN 1970, *GOODBYE COLUMBUS* opened, and 31-year-old Ali MacGraw became an overnight sensation. When she starred in *Love Story* the following year she became an international mega-star and remained one of the top ten movie box office draws for over five years. Although she made several more movies, Ali's personal life always came first and at the peak of her professional career she gave it up to marry macho Steve McQueen, with whom she'd starred in *The Getaway.*

Born on 1 April 1938 in Westchester County, New York, Ali worked her way through Wellesley College. Chosen in her sophomore year to be the summer guest editor of *Mademoiselle* magazine, Ali appeared on the August 1958 cover, fetchingly attired in pleated culottes and a sweater, and was signed by the prestigious Ford agency. Having been sketched in the nude by the surrealist Salvador Dali she was discovered for the movies and began her acting career in the 1968 film *A Lovely Way to Die.*

I first met Ali in Acapulco where she was honeymooning with her new husband, producer Bob Evans. She was a dazzling, original beauty, tanned, tawny and tons of fun. In her trademark hippy head-scarves and ethnic baubles, bangles and beads, she was the definitive

> '**There's a whole new generation of extraordinary women who are doing great things. Most of them have had kids, run businesses, re-invented themselves, and they're being ignored by the media.'**

Dynasty, *1985*.

fashion-plate of the 1970s. The couple seemed terribly in love – who doesn't on honeymoon? – but then Ali and passionate romance have always gone hand in hand.

Bob and Ali had a son, Joshua, but she threw the luxurious life of a Beverly Hills matron and Hollywood superstar down the drain to marry McQueen. Her home life with the mercurial actor was nerve-racking. Abandoned by his mother, McQueen was

moody, untrusting and dangerous, so his pathological distrust of women did not make for happy families. Both of them soon started hitting the bottle heavily.

Six tumultuous years later their marriage ended and Ali's professional and personal life hit rock bottom. With the failure of *Players* and a number of other films she made in the early 80s, Ali started using cocaine and continued drinking even more heavily. To make ends meet she worked as an interior designer and embarked on a series of unsatisfactory affairs.

In 1982 she played the lead in the mini series *Winds of War*. Ali gave a realistic and sympathetic performance which was slated by the critics – extremely cruelly, I thought. This caused her such grief that she promptly went on a week-long drinking spree.

Three years later Ali joined the cast of *Dynasty* as Lady Ashley Mitchell. When we lunched together on her first day of shooting, she was utterly petrified. Her bad reviews still haunted her and although I assured her that I believed, as did the *Dynasty* producers, that she had talent, she was as nervous as a prom queen. Unfortunately Ali was let go at the end of that season, another victim of the infamous 'Moldavian Massacre'.

Finally seeing the light, Ali checked herself into rehab – the Betty Ford Clinic – and she came out triumphantly several months later, cured of her addiction.

ON A CRISP SUNNY May afternoon Ali bounded into my LA apartment, still tanned and tawny and looking amazingly young for a woman who had just celebrated her sixtieth birthday.

We greeted each other affectionately and started talking as though it hadn't been three years since we'd last met. She's still frank, funny and endearingly self-deprecating, but she has so much more self-confidence now. We began talking about women's problems right away.

'There are so many fabulous, what I call grown-up women today,' she said. 'What amazes me is that the media hasn't caught onto that yet. They're still obsessed with having actors over 50 starring with 29-nine-year-old actresses.'

'That's the problem with being an actress in today's Hollywood,' I said.

'But it's *not* the problem, it's a mind-set. It's up to *us* to re-invent and change that mentality because this country *feeds* on what they're thrown. *People Magazine* or prime time television makes me want to slit my throat. It's not sour grapes to say there's a whole new generation of extraordinary women who are doing great things. Most of them have had kids and now they run businesses, re-invented themselves, and are ignored by the media,' she said.

'When the Lana Turner/Ava Gardner generation were in their late thirties, they were considered over the hill,' I said. 'Today, Sharon Stone is 40 and there are many women that age who are still considered youthful. The age boundary has moved forward at *least* fifteen if not twenty years.'

'Don't forget we are all so much healthier than we used to be. Fifty years ago the whole nutrition and exercise thing didn't exist,' said Ali.

'I wonder whether the younger generation of women today are going to be as fit as us when *they* get into *their* forties, fifties and sixties,' I mused.

'Because their life-style, the way they eat and the way they've become so acceptingly overweight is incredibly unhealthy,' said Ali. 'Is it just an American phenomenon?'

'It's happening everywhere,' I answered. 'I suppose it started with fast food, which I believe is basically putting poison into your system. As a kid I didn't eat a lot of sweets, biscuits and fatty stuff. I basically had a somewhat deprived diet but it was a *healthy* one. Today everybody's fighting fat, which seems like a tragedy to me.'

'Forty-five per cent of American women are overweight,' said Ali. 'They're probably not eating too much, just eating totally wrong.'

'And why are so many more people getting cancer?' I asked.

'Because the air is foul and the environment... Do you sit in the sun anymore?' she asked.

I nodded. 'I used to be a sun junkie and I'm

now paying the price with a lot of spots and freckles. The sun relaxes me but I don't go mahogany coloured anymore, I get splotchy. It might be age spots, but I think it's pollution from our atmosphere,' she said. 'What we're *not* told by our politicians and big business is utterly terrifying... in the end it's all about money,' Ali said. 'Look what they've just done in India – they've let off two underground nuclear bombs. All the villagers nearby have now got burns on their faces, nosebleeds, diarrhoea. Their politicians don't really *care* about their people much, but I believe that there's a tremendous amount of cynicism in the world and we're *all* expendable.'

We talked at length about this subject, then I asked, 'How do you take care of your face?'

'I wash my face several times a day with very fine granules, almond or something, then I put on moisturiser which contains sun-block and vitamin C extract. I have facials because I believe in deep cleansing. I drink lots of water but I wish that I didn't have so many little lines. You don't have lines, Joan,' Ali said. 'Why?'

'Maybe because I've always worn foundation,' I said. 'I was told by a friend when I was 21, *never* put your face in the sun if you don't want to look like a crocodile when you're 40. I was always tanning, but then I swore I'd *never* put my face in the sun again. I can see the difference now between my face and the rest of my body.'

'I have lines because I talk with my face like crazy, and living in Santa Fe is a scary deal because it's so dry. Maybe vanity will make me leave, because we're all turning into iguanas,' Ali laughed.

'Do you use hot or cold water on your face?' I asked.

'I fill a basin with lukewarm water and lavender oil, then I take a white washcloth so I can see when it's clean, and I put the washcloth over my face and deep-breathe into it. Lavender's so relaxing, it's *divine*. Next I put on moisturiser, and heavy duty vitamin C cream, then once a day I scrub my face clean. It only takes five minutes. Once in a while I do a papaya and enzymes mask.'

'I've always envied your great hair,' I said.

'It isn't good hair. It's healthy and shining but it looks *fatter* than it really is. I'd love to have a lion's mane. I colour it and try to keep it covered. I don't really know how to do my hair and that's why I loved it when it was really short, but there again I like it long too, because I can always put it back in a rubber band.'

I asked her what she thought about the media's image of today's beauty.

'Fashion magazines are the culprits, because they're hiring 15-year-olds now... it enrages me because *nobody* has a body like that unless they're between 15 and 21. The kids *look* divine but even liposuction, starvation or surgery can never *possibly* recreate their look. *Who* can look like that? It's hard for many women to be comfortable with themselves when these are the images that they're constantly subjected to,' she said.

'Interesting that we're both wearing black jeans and black T-shirts today,' I observed.

'Because it's the only thing I've got! Lately I've started to do Chinese drag, because it's chic and lasts forever. *Really* skinny trousers and antique silk things. I'm going to sit out this fashion moment. I'm not wearing fat cloggy combat shoes and slip dresses, because I look like a hooker. When I lost all my possessions in a fire it made me think: 'How many black suits did I really *need*?' I now only have a few terrific Armani suits, some of them really old, and my Chinese drag. Maybe it doesn't turn heads as much but it suits the way I live.'

'But you turn heads anyway, Ali,' I said.

'Well, you're very kind, but there was a period in my life, when I was 18 or 20, when I did the costume bit and I realise now that I wanted to be looked at *big* time,' she smiled. 'Now it's about finding stuff that you love, that you know really suits you. Your body changes from one day to the next so you've got to have a variety of stuff. There are days when I feel fat and I'm not gonna do bulimia as an alternative, so here come the Chinese shirt and skinny

'I'm going to sit out this fashion moment. I'm not wearing fat cloggy combat shoes and slip dresses, because I look like a hooker.'

pants, because my legs are still good.'

'How do you keep in such good shape?' I asked.

'I do yoga and Pilates four times a week and I walk my dogs,' she said. 'I love Pilates, and it's fabulous for you. I started when my son was born, which was twenty-seven years ago, to get rid of my stomach and to get my body back. Frankly I never had a better body, because Pilates elongates all your muscles and helps you breathe. I loathe the gym. I can't put on my spandex number and listen to the top ten and hang out in the shower room – it just makes me apoplectic,' she said. 'I also do yoga, either at a studio or on my own. I became seriously involved in yoga about six years ago as a way to reduce stress. It doesn't require any special or expensive equipment. All you need is an open mind and a desire to learn.

'It also lengthens and strengthens the muscles, without putting undue stress on them. It gives mature women the benefit of rigorous exercise without the excessive pounding and beating of traditional aerobics. It's a real turn-off when I see those narcissistic creatures flying around totally obsessed with their bodies. I think real sexuality is so much *more* than just the body and we don't *know* that until we're older. If all one has to offer is the perfect body it's just a crashing bore.'

'Are you faddy about diet?' I asked.

'I *can't* diet because I'm a brat.' She laughed. 'I don't do pills and all that rubbish. I need to eat three or four times a day. I can't do starvation. I'm very hyper and very nervous so I eat breakfast and I eat something in the middle of the day because otherwise I'm gonna go for the things I love most in the world, which is sugar and dough.' She laughed again. 'Preferably that translates into chocolate chip cookies or something thick and gooey, because I get narcoleptic by four o'clock if I haven't eaten. I try not to eat a huge dinner, but I *love* to eat, so it really depends on my social life. If I'm having a fabulous time I want a fabulous dinner but then I have to work it off. I cannot do the fabulous dinner and go to bed because that's deadly, but if I go dancing or carry on with someone... .'

She grinned mischievously so I asked her if she had anybody in her life now.

'I have a terrific man in my life, he's dramatically younger than I. I'm definitely *not* interested in some appropriately wealthy guy who's ready to retire. I would rather jump out of the window – and anyway they only like 28-year-old trophy dates. He's a musician on a ship so he goes away for three months at a time. It's very sexy and it works. I'm impossible, so how *brilliant* for me to have the run of doing everything that I want to. I'm also monogamous, so it's not like I'm screwing around in the age of

Photographed by Eddie Sanderson at Joan's LA apartment, 22 May 1998.

Aids like I was during my twenties. I'm older, and I *don't* want to do that dance. I want to *say* what I want and be with somebody who says "How terrific to have a wonderful time doing it". Our relationship has gone on for a few years and we have a fabulous time when we see each other. I think how amazingly lucky I am that I don't have to answer to *anybody*. I also have good heterosexual men friends,' she added.

'In that case I'm going to send all my single girlfriends to Santa Fe,' I joked.

'Don't you find as you get older that the value of *real* friendship is *so* staggeringly important?' she said. 'After one is blessed with health, of course.'

'Absolutely. Health is number one, family is number two. I've got rid of several friends recently, people who were drains. Stay with the people who warm you up. If I'm going to warm somebody I want to be warmed by them, too,' I said.

'So do I. I don't want to give my quantum energy out and be left with my tongue hanging out. I have hideously powerful energy and I want it back. My phonebook was burned in the fire and when something like that happens you *really* discover the people you want to connect with, because if somebody's desperate to find you, they will,' she said. 'I'm finding it harder and harder to be with big groups of people unless I choose everyone individually.

'I'm discovering that what I *don't* want to be anymore is resentful and judgmental. I think I was born in a little black robe with a perfectly pressed wig waiting in my cradle. Other people had christening suits – I had a judge's costume,' she laughed.

I asked her who her heroines were and she said, 'Betty Ford is one. 'She's an extraordinary woman. She's beautiful, feminine, real. She's very soft yet she's done such an *extraordinary* thing for hundreds of thousands of people, especially women, and she had a great marriage, with great children – that impossible juggling act that we've attempted ourselves.'

'You don't drink alcohol any more since you

'Don't you find as you get older that the value of real friendship is so staggeringly important?'

left the clinic?' I asked.

'I'm now violently allergic to it.'

I asked her if she'd like to say anything about the clinic and she thought carefully and then said truthfully:

'I went to the Betty Ford Clinic because I'd bottomed out. Seeing myself as a has-been in a business in which I'd once been the flavour of the month just added to my envy and rage. My best trick was to get right into *another* person's problems thus avoiding tackling my own; only now I realise that the whole manoeuvre was a device to make me feel powerful. All my life I'd chosen to go for 'Perfect' – even if it had been constipating and joyless. When was the last time I'd experienced true joy? Only in bed I'm afraid, and that's probably why I was so des-

perate for that connection – if I can make love then I can experience at least a *facsimile* of joy. I was drinking to loosen up, because when I was drunk I could dance, laugh, over-eat and be irresponsible. Underneath I was ashamed of my promiscuous and immoral behaviour. I'd been brought up with ethics and decency and I hated myself for having been involved in an adulterous relationship. After two weeks at Betty Ford I had to stand up in a meeting and talk to the rest of the patients. I said "My name is Ali, and I am an alcoholic-slash-male-dependent." The people in my group gave me *so* much and I felt I would just have to rebuild my life differently.'

She sipped her water and a far-away look came into her eyes.

'I was there for almost a month and enjoyed the kind of total honesty and vulnerability with perfect strangers that I realised is almost more intimate than anything I have with many of my "old friends". After I left I thanked God every day that I went into treatment and that I was able to get sober and get *cured*. Because alcoholism is a disease...'

I was curious to know what this woman who had worked so hard, had changed her life so totally and was so independent, would need on a desert island.

'For cosmetic vanity I'd want something to keep me from turning into a wrinkled old toad. Because I'd want to walk around naked in and out of the water,' she joked. 'I'd take some incredible moisturising sun protector that would work on my face and body. I always wear a pareo. Who needs clothes? I like large wads of fabric tied around me. It's comfortable, it's sexy and nobody can see what's underneath, especially on a bad day, except for the arms. I'm not crazy about the upper arms as I get older.'

'Do you do exercises for your upper arms?' I asked.

'It's too late, I should have started in my twenties,' she joked.

I asked Ali her views on make-up.

'With make-up all my lines get accentuated – the foundation goes into all my crevices and I break out in spots. I do spot cover stuff, and obviously I put it on when I work, but I cannot *wait* to take it off because it makes me look ten years older,' she said.

'Don't you wear any make-up at all?' I asked.

'I put my eyes on and I cover tons of my brown spots from the sun... with my green skin I can't have a peel because I'd end up with a face like a baby's bottom and a neck that doesn't match!' she laughed.

'You have wonderful olive skin,' I said.

'I'd like to be one of the Nigerian olives rather than one of the green ones!' she giggled.

'On the beach, do you wear a sun hat? And what factor protection?' I asked.

'I'm told that over fifteen makes no difference. You just have to keep doing factor fifteen every fifteen minutes because it doesn't last. Sometimes I wear a hat because I colour my hair and it turns this disgusting brassy red if I don't. *This* part of being over 40 is a real *pain* in the ass – this whole vanity maintenance – not waking up with wonderful grey roots, brass-red dried stick-like hair and a red nose takes a *lot* of work.'

We both laughed at Ali's self-deprecating attitude. 'But you've got such a great attitude towards everything, you're so honest about your problems,' I said.

'I have to be honest with you; I'm – I think the word is *dismayed*, when I find myself in any situation where tiny perfect little 18-year-olds

'Now I realise if you watch what you eat, you'll look terrific, but if you don't you'll be a blimp. It's a bore. I'd like to have an ice-cream soda right now!'

are running around in bikinis with no make-up and perfect hair. That was *us* once Joan!' Ali laughed.

'Ah, but will they look as good as *us* when they get to our age?' I asked.

'That's true but *they* don't know it. I must admit I feel sadder and vainer than I thought I was going to be at this age. I always took my fitness and health for granted and never realised what menopause does to a woman's body. They always talked about the moods, flushes and the rages – I never got any of that, but I didn't expect to become so food sensitive. If I eat too much bread or sugar my stomach spreads and *nobody* told us that could happen. Now I realise if you watch what you eat, you'll look terrific, but if you don't you'll be a blimp. It's a *bore*. I'd like to have an ice-cream soda *right now*!' she said.

'If I have more than three glasses of red wine, my face becomes a blancmange,' I admitted.

'My downfall is bread. For me the sugar in yeast and bread is the same as wine. For centuries, we've seen *staggeringly* dishy-looking, rounded women in paintings who would not make the cover of *Vogue* today. Why? Because they've got a *tummy*. That's what's so hot about this movie with Sonia Braga, called *Tiete*. She has great, beautiful breasts, a big, big ass and she makes *no* attempt to look like a kid... She's a *woman* and she spends the movie with a 19-year-old altar boy. It's divine and funny, and it's a celebration of womanhood. Hollywood could not *imagine* making it.'

'Have you stopped acting now?' I asked her.

'By public demand,' she laughed.

'That is extraordinary, because you were the number one female box office star in the 70s.'

'Don't you think a lot of that is driven by personality?' she said. 'There's a moment when everything comes together – my miracle vehicle was *Love Story*.'

'You were the face of that time... You were

totally modern then, but you're totally modern now. You have the look of today,' I said.

She laughed again. 'I've been wearing a black T-shirt and jeans for twenty years. It's not exactly ground-breaking,'

'In Acapulco, when we had dinner on your honeymoon, you had the turbans and silk scarves from India and exotic earrings and bracelets. I wondered who had the most bracelets, you or me?'

We discussed fashion, then Ali said, 'You know, pop celebrity is funny. Some people have staggering talent and never get their moment. I've had right moments and right times, but when the reviews started to get really vile, it took courage to endure because it's like a public testing. When I did *Winds of War* it was a very sad, scary, humiliating time for me. I also married two hugely powerful Hollywood figures who lived a life that people considered tabloid fodder.

'I'm glad I was in my thirties and early forties when my success happened, because if I'd had that huge moment and then that huge fall, I think I'd be either a drug addict or in the nut house now. But *Love Story* gave me those unbelievable choices and a tremendous entrée. Once I got through Delhi airport in twenty seconds because the immigration guy had seen *Love Story*!

'I make documentaries but I haven't acted for ages. I'd rather make my money selling a lipstick or go to fabulous places and decorate or write. I want to travel and be with people who talk about something other than what an episode of *ER* is doing in the ratings.'

I suddenly realised we'd talked for hours and Eddie was getting restless. Like a couple of naughty schoolgirls we giggled our way through the photo session. Ali has such a disarming honesty as well as an infectious charm. At 60 she seems to have truly re-discovered herself. She likes what she's found – and so did I.

SHIRLEY MACLAINE

MULTI-TALENTED LEGEND

D**RIVING TOWARDS** S**HIRLEY** M**ACLAINE'S** house in Malibu on one of the worst days of the El Nino storms, I could barely see through the windscreen for the teeming rain. Mud slides had turned the Pacific Coast Highway into a terrifying obstacle course, and backed up the traffic for miles.

But inside Shirley's charming beach house, where she has lived for many years, the atmosphere was warm and inviting. Shirley, casual in blue jeans, cowboy boots, cashmere sweater and a silk scarf was wearing no make-up, and we sat in front of her fire, sipping coffee and watching the huge white waves pounding the beach, then breaking at the foundations of her house.

I've known Shirley for over thirty years, as we both started our Hollywood movie careers at the same time. Her first starring role, in *The Trouble With Harry*, was coincidentally opposite my old nemesis Blake Carrington, AKA John Forsythe.

Born Shirley Maclaine Beatty, the eldest child of two schoolteachers, she was dancing and singing from the age of three. Shirley was thrust into stardom when she understudied

Carol Haney on Broadway in *The Pajama Game*. When Shirley went on, she drew the attention of the legendary producer Hal Wallis, who immediately signed her to a Paramount Pictures contract.

Shirley's career took off rapidly. She soon became one of Hollywood's brightest young stars, as well as the only female member of the Rat Pack – the legendary coterie of wise-cracking cronies which included Frank Sinatra, Dean Martin, Sammy Davis Jnr. and Peter Lawford.

She married Broadway producer Steve Parker in 1954 and had one daughter, Sashi. Their marriage was unconventional to say the least. Parker lived most of his time in Japan and the couple, although close, spent little time together, eventually divorcing in 1980.

Shirley won an Academy Award for Best Actress in 1984 for *Terms of Endearment*, after receiving nominations for *Some Came Running, The Apartment, Irma La Douce*, and *Turning Point*. She is a multi-talented woman. She acts, sings, dances, produces, travels and takes an active part in human causes. She has also written eight internationally best-selling books, and Shirley does all these things with equal expertise.

When she was still in her forties Shirley told me that she was 'ageing up' to play 60- and 70-year-olds: 'That way I'll be first in the running for all the best old dame roles when I finally hit that age,' she grinned.

In the early sixties Shirley was almost my sister-in-law, when I was engaged to her brother Warren Beatty. As I was a Fox contractee we would visit Shirley on the set of *Can-Can*. Shirley was then, as she still is, quirky, funny and unconventional, with the same cute freckles and gamine mop of short red hair and, even now in her sixties, her lithe dancer's body has barely changed at all.

After reminiscing, I told Shirley that I thought it was fantastic that she was now directing.

'Directing is such an on-the-job experience,' she said. 'What I want is to follow through my vision from the beginning to the end, and not watch somebody else make a wrong decision. It's nice to find that you're not a control freak but that you just want to fulfil your own vision, it's a big difference. I've spent the last year raising the money, which when you're out of the studio system is really difficult.'

I sympathised, as I was due to be in a film later this year if the producers could raise the funds.

Photographed for* Life *magazine, Hollywood, 1961.

'It's *always* a problem,' Shirley sighed. 'But I *believe* in *Bruno*. It's a really wonderful script, and I'm going to play a good little part. It's an ensemble piece. I'm still interested in acting, no doubt about that, Joanie, I'm not *ever* going to give it up.'

'But haven't you found that as an actress gets older it becomes much more difficult to get good roles?' I said.

'You have to give up the vanity; if you have too much of that actressy stuff it's difficult. It *has* to go. Character parts are usually *much* richer, more alive and much more colourful.'

'I agree. I'm playing a character part for the first time in *A Clandestine Marriage* with Nigel Hawthorne. It's the sort of part that some actresses I know would kill for...' Shirley poured us more coffee as the sea raged stronger, and I said, 'Shirley, so *many* women admire you tremendously, for your talent, originality, spirit, and your belief in the afterlife. But it's something that very few people seem to *really* understand. I wonder if you could tell me a little about where you developed that from.'

'I don't know where that came from, but I think I've probably been a mystic since I was very small. I remember those feelings, *knowing* there was something *more* to what we think is everything. The search and the adventure on the trail of what it may or may *not* mean has been a lot of fun. And I *love* to have fun! I think with ageing you get a sense that there is another dimensional truth, that it's as real as the life around us. It's called going internally, and when you *start* going internally that's where the real journey begins. Yeats said that the only journey worth taking is the one within oneself. Poets usually do get to this, and some older people certainly do. Einstein got to it – he just knew that there was more because so many of the things they discover scientifically come from an internal dream, from imagination, or from a place inside *themselves*.'

'So do you believe that your mind can *control* your destiny?' I asked.

'I think we are all in control of our destiny and it's not so much listening to the mind as to the *soul* and to the consciousness. When you start getting in touch with this stuff you realise that *everything* that happens to you, regardless of *how* painful it might prove, is really for the good, and creates more harmony. It gives you inner peace.'

'You've written many books about previous lifetimes, so you must often feel as if you've been somewhere and done something before.'

'Yes, I've had a lot of *déja vu*,' she smiled.

'You've certainly been fulfilling your own vision practically all your life. You *always* seem to have done what you wanted.'

'That's for sure,' she said and I asked Shirley if she was involved with anyone right now.

'I'm finished with that part of my life, Joanie. I don't particularly feel the need for a partner – I have so many partners in myself,' she laughed.

'I don't just mean sex. Don't you miss the cuddling, the sharing, the intimate contact?' I asked.

'I have so much intimacy with my friends. I think you can be more intimate and deeper on many levels with friends than if you have a partner you're always worrying about,' she said.

'I think that women spend too much of their creative lives worrying about their lover, their romantic life or their children – I know I did. It really side-tracked my creativity and work motivation for years,' I said.

Shirley agreed as she sipped her coffee. The sky was darkening from the rain as we spoke, even though it was only three o'clock. I asked her how she relaxed and de-stressed.

'It's essential to me to live in an environment that's peaceful. That's why I live at the beach, right on the water, which comes right under my house – and a lot further than that today!'

Huge waves shook the foundations. 'Living here *does* have its disadvantages in terms of timing and cancelled appointments, as well as rock slides and back-up of traffic. Today it almost seems apocalyptic, but I love it. *Wherever* I go I want to see trees and birds – I *have* to see nature because otherwise I feel cranky and totally out of alignment. I also do my Chi Gong every single morning.'

I asked her about Chi Gong and she said, 'Chi means life energy and Gong means movement, so I stand in the centre of myself and let my body move where it wants to move, and that aligns the energy. I can feel it happen.'

'Is this your basic exercise routine, then?'

Shirley chuckled, 'I'm getting lazier and lazier as the years go by.'

'But surely you exercise at the gym and still do barre work?' I asked.

'Oh my God *no*, Joanie. I *couldn't* get through it. I wouldn't even *want* to.' She shook her head. 'There's one machine at the gym that works the upper and the lower body, and I'll go there if nobody else is around, but I can't take all this macho testosterone that floats around. It makes me sick.'

We both laughed. 'I know,' I said, 'because it doesn't matter *how* much you work out, after a certain age you're *never* going to have a tight young body. I know a 50-year-old woman who

Photographed in New York, 13 November 1990.

Terms of Endearment, *1983.*

'I think that we are all born to our parents for a reason and so I feel that we choose our parents. What you need to do is then look at why.'

kick-boxes, runs for two hours and does aerobics *every* day. By the time she's 65 she'll probably have severe arthritis because we're not *meant* to do that to our bodies.'

'Oh, she'll have serious problems working that hard, there's no question about it. I believe that exercise shouldn't be stressful. You can *make* yourself stressed out by doing too much. I won't do that anymore. I'm listening to my body and it doesn't *want* to.'

'You probably listen to your body in terms of what you eat, as well. Although you look as though you're about the same weight as when we first met,' I said.

'I have gained weight but lately I've been on a fast. I didn't do it for weight really. I did it for my health. Fasting for cosmetic reasons or vanity is quite the wrong approach, and in my opinion *everything* is a question of intent. So I think about what is better for me relating to my *health*, rather than relating to my mirror. After my health is balanced again, I'll fast for seven

days on nothing but apple juice. And it's *remarkable*, Joan. My God.' She looked incredibly enthusiastic and showed me the backs of her hands, which were notably free from marks or spots. 'The liver spots on my hands decreased by about 75%, and all the aches and pains that I was beginning to suffer went away, and my need for food decreased. We all eat *far* too much anyway. In Europe what I would miss is the wine and the great bread and patés, but I don't think I'd be able to indulge in those fabulous meals now. I'm just going to listen to my body,' she said firmly.

'So sometimes you'll eat meat if you feel like it, or cookies. Is there *nothing* that you wouldn't eat?' I asked.

'Because I'm a sugar freak the only thing that I do is to stay away from it. I don't eat red meat – my body doesn't want it, but it *does* want fish and chicken, and then vegetables, although not as much fruit. It's the alkaline system that you want to maintain, *not* the acidic.

And we all eat *far* too much salt, which is a killer,' she said.

'As a red-head you have delicate skin so do you have a particular skin care routine?'

'I don't do anything except stay out of the sun,' she said, 'I wash my face with soap and water, period, and I don't even use moisturiser.'

I told her it was amazing that she had such good skin considering she did so little, and she grinned. 'I never have so why start now?' I then asked her about make-up.

'I don't use make-up except to cover up tiny blemishes. I would *never* put a full base on my face. God, I would feel like I couldn't breathe. Of course I have to when I'm working but I hate it.'

I asked Shirley what she would take if she was wrecked on a desert island and could only bring one inanimate thing with her. She thought for a long minute, then said, 'I did this Santiago di Compostela Camino pilgrimage two years ago – and I got in touch with how *little* we really need. I'm tempted to say if I was allowed one thing on a desert island it would be a good pair of shoes,' she laughed. 'It's what grounds us to the earth. Feet are what protect us.'

I then asked her about her heroes and she said instantly: 'Gandhi and Jesus and *definitely* Mother Teresa.'

'Do you feel that young people today have fewer heroes and heroines than we did?' I asked.

'Oh yeah, I think the disintegration of human values is so rapid. We have very few modern heroes. It's hard to live up to what you think you can be today because there are so few role models.'

'I think that young people's values today have changed so much from our generation. I'm horrified by the values of young children. They need constant stimulation. They're bored. I am sure you were never bored?' I asked.

'That's really true. And I am *never* bored now. I'll always find something interesting even if it's watching an ant crawl across a piece of sand. I don't know what boredom's all about – I'm just eternally curious,' she said.

'You probably have your parents to thank for that. It should be every parent's responsibility to make their children aware of the world.'

'Dad was certainly that way, he was so curious about everything. Mother was rather withholding, as you know, and I think that made me curious, because I didn't know what she was thinking. I always knew what Dad was thinking but not Mother. I also think that we are all born to our parents for a reason and so I feel that we *choose* our parents. What you need to do is then look at *why*. Look at the lessons you learned from them and all the inspiration you got from them,' she said.

She offered me more coffee but I said I had to leave before the Pacific Coast Highway became impassable and I became the woman who came to dinner. She laughed and said, 'I like to live in Malibu because I love nature and part of that is the excesses.'

'You are amazing, Shirley.' 'I am,' she said. I started to leave as I knew she had to go to the market. 'You look wonderful; fulfilled and grounded.'

Shirley opened the front door, a blast of rain and wind almost knocking us down, and we made arrangements to meet again when I was next in LA.

Shirley is a multi-talented woman – her feet planted firmly on the ground, while her imagination is a potent force that constantly drives her to seek new challenges.

Age cannot wither her
Nor custom stale
Her infinite variety.

ANTHONY AND CLEOPATRA, WILLIAM SHAKESPEARE

MICHELLE PHILLIPS

ALL-AMERICAN MAMA

MICHELLE PHILLIPS LIVES IN a small unpretentious semi-detached bungalow in the Cheviot Hills just behind the golf course near Fox Studios. It was a beautiful May afternoon and she had been reading in a comfy chaise longue on her patio. She greeted me totally without make-up, her pale skin scrubbed clean, her clear blue eyes sparkling with humour, blonde hair short and casually arranged. Wearing black cotton pants, a loose white shirt and black boots, the former Mamas and Papas singer was extremely relaxed and full of gentle *joie de vivre*.

At 53, Michelle, a fellow Gemini, has a girlishly endearing air, and talks frankly about most subjects. She started her career as a teenaged model, then found fame in the mid-60s as the gorgeous counterpart to the corpulent Mama Cass in the hot rock-folk group the Mamas and the Papas. They were the

rage of their time, creating scandal and controversy until Cass died in 1974, at only 29.

Michelle married the group's lead singer, John Phillips, they had a daughter Chynna; then, after their divorce, Michelle became Hollywood's reigning love goddess. Turbulent affairs with Roman Polanski, Jack Nicholson and Warren Beatty culminated in a week-long marriage to the hell-raising, heavy drinking actor Dennis Hopper. They met in 1966 married on Hallowe'en and separated a week later. 'We called it the Six Day War,' smiled Michelle.

In the 70s she became a movie star, playing most memorably opposite Rudolf Nureyev in Ken Russell's *Valentino,* tantalising audiences with glimpses of her fabulous nude body in the daring love scenes. Other not so memorable films followed until she landed the role of head vixen in *Knots' Landing.* During this era Michelle, Morgan Fairchild in *Flamingo Road* and I in *Dynasty* would often battle it out for the title of Best Bitch on television.

Settling onto the sofa in her cosy cluttered living room we sipped Evian water and I got straight down to the nitty gritty:

'Didn't you have a long relationship with Jack Nicholson?'

'I eat everything I want but I only eat small portions and that's the trick.'

Michelle grinned her pixie grin. 'Trouble with Jack is when he goes on location he always wants to screw around. It's tough having a relationship with a guy like that.'

'So going with Warren Beatty right after him must have been like jumping from the frying pan into the fire?' I asked.

'Well, you should know,' Michelle giggled. 'Weren't you engaged to him?'

'*Before* he became a star. Now *don't* change the subject, Michelle. You have really good skin and you're not wearing any make-up, are you?' I asked.

'Just a little,' she admitted.

'Well, it's cleverly done. What's your beauty routine?'

'The most important part of my routine is to actually do the forty splashes thing *every* single morning and every single night. Erno Laszlo got me into that thirty years ago. You fill the bowl with hot water, not scalding but nice and hot, then you wash your face with Erno Laszlo's soap. You lean your head over the bowl and you splash one, two, three, four. It is actually a deep pore cleanser and it gets in there and cleans your skin. Then I pat my face and use a very light toner applied with cotton wool, clean it off, then put on moisturiser. I'm currently using Paul Mitchell white oak cleanser which is very mild – I use a lot of his products, but his white oak cleanser and moisturisers are great for my skin. Erno said that you should do your

splashes as religiously as saying your prayers, that it should be almost a spiritual experience to clean your face and I really responded to that.'

'How religious about this are you?' I asked.

'It doesn't matter *how* many margharitas or martinis I've had, nor what I've done, or *who's* waiting for me, I still do it every night.' She grinned.

I know that since the 1940s some of the world's greatest beauties have used Hungarian Erno Laszlo's products, which are still available from Saks in New York and Harrods in London. 'Although I don't use all of his stuff,' continued Michelle, 'I still use the cream at night and on my eyes, hands and lips.' She went into the bathroom and came back with a pot. 'This is it. It's called active phelatal. When I'm working I do the full slap and drag. I use a Prescriptives base, powder over that, then a little eye-shadow. I crimp my lashes, and apply a good mascara – Long Lash Maybelline mascara. It's the best there is, and it's *cheap*.'

'Don't you think that many really expensive beauty products don't actually work that well?' I asked.

'Sure. You can buy just as good a product for four bucks at the drug store as you can for forty in the department store. That stuff from La Femme is cheap as dirt, and I *love* their eye shadows and powders, because they're natural colours, and they do a great taupe blusher.'

I asked her what she did for her hair.

'It's very fine, so I use Paul Mitchell wash, rinse and sculpting foam. It gives it body, and I keep it short these days because I *kill* it with hot rollers when I'm filming which is the worst thing for hair.'

'It's better for your hair to use foam rollers and wait until they dry,' I said. 'Or do what our grandmothers did – sleep with our hair in rag curlers – real passion killers!'

'No thank you!' Michelle laughed.

'Do you have an exercise routine? You're in such good shape.'

'I do one exercise every morning when I'm in the shower. Want to see it?'

She stood up, stretched to the ceiling, bent forward, and touched her toes.

'How many times?'

'Once,' she said mischievously.

'That's it?' I asked incredulously.

'Yup. That's it. That's *all* I do.'

'You touch your toes *once* and you have this body? Women are going to hate you, Michelle.'

'Okay. Well I *do* walk my dog three times a *week*.'

'The poor mutt only goes walkies three times a *week*?'

'Well, I only walk her three or four times a week for an hour, pretty fast. But it's really good. It clears your head and wakes you up.'

'I can't *believe* that's all the exercise you do. You don't play sports – tennis?'

She giggled again and shook her head.

'You must eat a very modest diet then.'

'I eat *everything* I want but I only eat s[m]all portions and that's the trick. For lunch today [I] ate a bowl of pasta with cheese, cream and vodka, which I made myself, and asparagus. I eat lots of greens but not much meat. Although if I feel like it I'll have a huge steak.'

'And, if you feel like it, you'll also have a cookie or a cream cake or something fattening?'

'No, I don't have a sweet tooth. I have more of a deli taste than a bakery.'

'But you don't diet and there's nothing you won't eat?'

'I can't think of one thing I will not eat.'

'What about drinking?' I asked.

'Oh, I drink like a fish.' We both roared with laughter. 'I wouldn't *dream* of having a meal without a glass of wine.'

'Well, I certainly agree, and that's a *very* European attitude.'

'If I can't have a glass of wine with my food it's probably not worth eating.'

'So you'll drink wine at lunchtime?'

The Mamas and the Papas.

'The most important thing is for parents to educate children about the pitfalls of drugs and that's where we should be putting our money.'

Photographed by Eddie Sanderson in Michelle Phillips' garden, LA, 19 May 1998.

'Of *course*. I just did.'

'That's unusual for Americans.'

'They're missing out.'

'Do you smoke?'

'No, I gave it up. I just smoke pot now!'

I choked on my water. 'Still?'

'Yeah. Not a lot though and much less than I used to. It relaxes me, so if I feel like it I have a puff or two.'

'You think they should legalise it?' I asked.

'*Absolutely*. Legalise it for people who just want to smoke it and *definitely* legalise it for people who need it for pain relief. They should legalise the growing of hemp for a myriad of different products.'

'You don't think that young people who start off smoking joints will graduate to cocaine, and then to heroin? That's how we are indoctrinated against the idea of legalising cannabis,' I said.

'Well, I think everybody has to take responsibility for themselves, and to make it illegal only glorifies it. It mystifies marijuana – makes it appealing. The most important thing is for *parents* to educate children about the pitfalls of drugs and that's where we should be putting our money. I've never tried heroin in my life and *everybody* did cocaine in the 70s and 80s. So you either got over it or you didn't.'

'How old are your kids now?'

'Chynna is 30. God help me, remember little baby Chynna? She's married to Billy Baldwin.'

'So you're part of the Baldwin clan? You actually look a little like Kim Basinger, Alec Baldwin's wife.'

'Yes I know, I'm flattered,' she grinned.

'Do you take vitamins?'

'I take a good daily multi-vitamin, and then a thousand milligrams of C, a thousand of E, a little B complex, two amino acids and calcium.'

'Calcium's very important. Do you take HRT? Everybody I talk to over the age of 50 does.'

'I have an oestrogen patch, and the natural progesterone.'

I asked Michelle what she does to de-stress and relax.

'I have a lovely jacuzzi out back and I like to sit in it and read a lot. A martini is a great de-stresser, and half a bottle of wine's even better.'

'Do you ever mindlessly lie in bed channel-surfing and watching Jerry Springer and his bunch of idiots?' I asked.

'I watched Jerry Springer for the first time recently and I couldn't *believe* it! His show draws out the worst elements of our society. I've never seen an uglier group of people on or off that stage – even the audience who are cheering them on. What kind of trash gets off on that kind of misery?' she asked.

'Morons?' I ventured.

'It's a sad commentary on the public to think that's what entertains them. I was embarassed for anyone who'd go on that show knowing they were going to be humiliated,' she said.

'What *I* think is sad is the end of glamour on TV. The shows that we were doing in the 80s – *Knots Landing*, *Dynasty* and *Dallas*. We all looked so glamorous and women loved those shows… they were fairytale fantasies,' I said.

'I guess audiences don't want any more fantasies,' Michelle shrugged.

'Now Michelle, I know you're a very positive person so I'm sure that positive thinking plays an important role in your life.'

'Yes, it has from the time I was a child. I was always a very happy, positive child and so I was always a very happy, positive *adult*. It's just part of how I was genetically engineered. I've always been a very adventurous person and I've been lucky because I had a pretty face and a bubbly personality, and early on I found myself around intelligent people from whom I learned a lot. It makes you wonder how much of life is what you make of it, and how much is just sheer luck.'

'Right, but you were in a successful group

'**Whatever time you're given with somebody is grand, but if it's not to be, that's not the end of your life, it's the end of his life.**'

with Mama Cass, who was so fat and unhappy that she killed herself, didn't she?'

Michelle became quite agitated in her denial. 'No, no, Cass died of a heart attack.'

'She was quite the opposite of you, wasn't she? She over-ate and she was a depressive personality.'

'No, she wasn't depressed. That was the funny thing about Cass. She was a very positive and funny woman but there's no denying she had a lot of problems. I don't believe you can be grossly overweight in a society that frowns upon obesity and *not* have some kind of a problem about it. Nobody *wants* to be overweight – and Cass certainly didn't. She was always on diets, but there was stuff in her childhood that was always working against her. I really loved her. She was so talented.' I asked Michelle who were her heroines now.

'My mother died when I was five and I was already kind of a little scrapper. By the time I became a teenager I was out there scrapping on my own and I didn't admire many people. But I actively pursued people that I wanted to be with and I was always hanging out with older people. When I was 11 my first real friend was 19, but I can't think of anyone I consciously thought that I could emulate.'

'If you could take one beauty product to a desert island, an inanimate thing, what would it be?' I asked.

'Moisturiser and a *very* big book.'

'How important are sex and love to you?'

'I've been married three times and I wouldn't want to do *that* again. I've been with Jeff since 1987 and it's enormously important to me to have a happy home. I don't *need* the drama of being with a new guy. I don't want it and I don't thrive on it. I've always just looked for a happy home and someone who can provide that stable environment, who's there when you come home. I need the cosiness of love and family. We have two 16-year-olds.

Austin was 6 when Jeff and I got together, then the following year we adopted Aaron who was 7. It's hard having two teenage boys in the house, and sometimes I just can't deal with it. Then Jeff says, "It's all right, I'll take care of everything. And he does." '

'My God that's unusual. So many men don't want to have household responsibilities – they leave that up to the woman,' I said.

'Especially if they're not his children. Jeff is seven years younger than me, but it's not a big issue.'

'If Jeff left you or died do you think you'd find someone else?' I asked.

'Yes, because whatever time you're given with somebody is grand, but if it's not to be, that's not the end of your life, it's the end of *his* life,' she burst into peals of laughter.

'Some people think that women in their fifties or sixties shouldn't be sexual in any way – how do *you* feel about that?' I asked.

'I'm 53 and a bigger sex fiend than I ever was,' laughed Michelle. 'As I get older I become more sexual.'

'Why do you think that is?'

'I have no idea, it's just some kind of great hormone blast that I'm getting now. Let's not knock it,' she stood up and grinned. 'It's martini time!'

As we were photographed in her pretty garden with the frisky mutt I reflected that Michelle was a truly happy woman, a free spirit, committed to her man yet at peace with her life.

I marvelled at her ability to eat what she liked, to drink, smoke the occasional joint, do little or no exercise and yet still look fabulous.

So what can one learn from Michelle Phillips? To always be true to ourselves whatever happens. To eat, drink and be merry but be aware that over-indulgence can be detrimental to one's health and beauty. Michelle goes against a lot of the accepted rules but her rules definitely work for her.

THERE SEEM TO BE two kinds of American women today – super-fit and super-fat. Stefanie Powers fits into the former category perfectly. Tall and enviably slender she possesses the most fabulously toned derrière I've ever seen. Wearing a tight brown sweater and matching pants, her luxuriant red hair falling casually around her face, she welcomed me to her pretty house high in the Hills of Beverly. Although it was pouring with unseasonable rain the house was welcoming and cosy; there was a blazing log fire in the living room and classical music played softly in the background.

It was 6 o'clock on a cold California May evening and without preamble Stefanie went behind her exceedingly well-appointed oak bar and offered me a drink. We both had a glass of wine, then Stefanie lit up a small cigar, I a Marlboro, and we started talking.

I've known Stefanie for over twenty years and always admired the way she's been able to switch from movies, to TV, to the musical theatre with aplomb. The culmination of her career was as Jennifer Hart opposite Robert Wagner in the TV series *Hart to Hart*, a role which made Stefanie Powers a household name.

I'd recently worked with Stefanie and R.J. in a movie in Montreal and found her an exceedingly glamorous actress, blessed with talent, great humour and tremendous *joie de vivre*. She is also President of the William Holden Wildlife Foundation, a cause very dear to her heart.

'Acting and the Foundation are the two most important priorities in my life,' she said. 'I try not to let one suffer in favour of the other. So what suffers, invariably, is my personal life.'

She has been married for four years to French Count Patrick de la Chenais, but their diverse careers often keep them apart. 'I try to maintain a balance in my life,' she said, as we sipped our wine by the roaring fire. 'That's why I live between Beverly Hills and Kenya, the headquarters of the Foundation. I want to have my ashes scattered there.'

HEART TO HEART WITH
STEFANIE POWERS

Photographed by Eddie Sanderson at Stefanie Powers' house in Beverly Hills, 12 May 1998.

'If it's really well done, deep tissue massage gets the blood and all the liquids circulating and gets the toxins out.'

Stefanie's passion for animals began in her childhood. Born Stefania Federkiewicz, of Polish descent, one of her earliest ambitions was to become a veterinarian.

'Everyone would bring stray and injured animals to our house – because they knew we would care for them,' she smiled.

She recalls how her mother even once revived a white mouse which Stefanie had brought home, fearing it had frozen to death. 'Mother put the mouse in the oven and warmed it up,' she laughed. 'The mouse made a miraculous recovery.'

When Stefanie gave up her plans to become a vet in favour of acting, she did not abandon her love for animals. Her present menagerie includes two terriers and an Amazon parrot.

'My interest in animals has evolved into something I never would have imagined,' she says.

Divorced from actor Gary Lockwood, she met the handsome super-star William Holden in 1972 and they found a tremendous affinity with each other, thanks in part to their fascination with wild animals and travelling. In 1973, Holden brought Stefanie to Africa for the first time, anxious for the new woman in his life to see the continent that had become his obsession. He was her lover for nine years, and introduced her to the plight of wildlife.

Holden had just established the Mount Kenya Game Ranch to save Kenya's wildlife, setting up an animal orphanage and initiating a captive breeding programme to ensure that endangered species survived. The couple travelled and worked together extensively, and when Holden died in 1981, the following year Stefanie established the Foundation in his memory. 'We want to work in areas where not enough has been done,' she said at the launch. Seventeen years later it is still her enduring passion.

I asked her how she kept her amazing figure. 'You have the body of a 17-year-old, you really do. It's astounding.'

'It's playing polo,' she said.

'Lots of people play polo in England, but they don't have figures like yours,' I said.

'Well, I do yoga,' she admitted. 'It's very strenuous and athletic. It's done in a hot room so the body stays flexible and the muscles stay relaxed.'

'Well it obviously works because you have tiny hips, which is enviable,' I said.

'I used to dance and dancers' bodies have memories so if you start *young* the body remembers, and so do the muscles. The best exercise I do is Pilates. It covers everything.'

'I agree, when I did Pilates my body was the best it's ever been,' I said immodestly. 'Even after three children.'

'It's fabulous for stretching and tones you brilliantly.'

'Do you do special exercises for your butt?'

'It's important to do everything you can. Cross-training, cross-exercising, *whatever* you can. Deep tissue massage is also wonderful. The harder the better. It helps keep the circulation moving freely. If it's really well done, deep tissue massage gets the blood and all the liquids circulating *and* gets the toxins out,' she said.

'If you smoke and drink do you think that toxins build up in the body?' I asked.

Stefanie on her ranch with an Arabian foal.

Photographed with Robert Wagner on the set of Two Harts in Three-Quarter Time, Montreal, October 1995.

'A *life* builds up toxins in the body,' she laughed. 'So you get rid of the toxins by perspiring, that's why my yoga teacher has a hot room. A wonderful dietitian called Doctor Beever had a theory which makes a lot of sense. He talked about the body as being a great clearing factory, whose function was the division of the good and the bad that we put into it. It turns proteins into energy, other things get stored or processed through, and there's also garbage that needs to be cleaned out regularly. Dr Beever says that the body has the ability to flush everything out and that the skin, which is the largest organ in the body, is the body's first avenue for released toxins. If you perspire it does its job wonderfully.'

'You believe perspiration can get rid of all that?' I said. She nodded vigorously. 'But I can't perspire,' I said. 'I go bright red. Even when I was a kid playing volley ball I'd only get a little dew on my forehead.'

'Well, you must have done something right because your skin is fabulous. It has always had great luminosity and that's health!' Stefanie assured me.

'I know that you eat healthily and I also know you love wine. Don't you consider that far better for you than a Diet Coke?'

TUBE

Stefanie on the Kenyan ranch where the William Holden Foundation began.

'I'd *never* drink that! I get my sugar through wine,' laughed Stefanie. 'I'd rather that than a chocolate bar.'

'You obviously never eat junk food,' I said.

'I don't eat *anything* with a face!' she shuddered.

'Does that mean no chicken or fish?' I asked.

'*Especially* chicken. No meat, no poultry and *nothing* that's ever been farmed. Being a conservationist, you learn about all the awful things going on in the world of ecology. As a result, you tend not to eat many things you previously ate because of what's going on in the environment. Any *notion* of eating a crustacean, a carnivore that eats filth and garbage and lives along the coastline underwater on rocks is *out*. No wonder shrimp and lobster are the main causes of food poisoning,' added Stefanie. 'They're garbage collectors.'

As she refilled our glasses I asked her about her beauty routine.

'About the only thing I *try* to do regularly is to wear sunscreen, because I'm constantly in the sun and I know how the ozone level is diminishing. I've had skin cancer and it's no fun. I've had a big chunk of my neck taken out and bits removed, so sunscreen's *essential*. Sure it's fabulous to look tanned in the summertime, but fake it. Clarins make a great non-streaky tanning lotion that turns you a wonderful golden colour in a few hours. It's good for legs and arms and body. It doesn't dry out the skin, it lasts about three, four days and it *really* works.'

I asked Stefanie what make-up she was wearing now and she replied, 'I use a French powder which is yellow and somehow never looks cakey, and Prescriptives make-up for work.'

We talked about how busy Stefanie was with many different projects and I asked her what she did to de-stress and to relax.

She said, 'Exercise, exercise. Because it *focuses.* Exercise for me represents many things. It represents cleansing – so it's health – and it's also anti-stress. I find that when I exercise and sweat, in the sense that an animal sweats, I feel *so* much better. I asked a doctor why sensible, successful people take up this absurd game called polo as a sport, because it's enormously difficult and dangerous, and it can be expensive depending upon what level you play it. What is it that makes it so addictive? When the game finishes all anybody can think about is the next game. He said he believed it was physiological – the combination of adrenalin and endorphins. We know that endorphins are exhibited at a certain point in strenuous exercise and endorphins kick in and push you through the barrier of pain and into euphoria. Polo combines that with adrenalin, because it's a challenge and a battle, the things which aggressive human nature needs to exhibit and direct. As a result, polo seems to have a very healthy effect on me.'

'So when you play you feel really relaxed?' I asked.

'Absolutely,' she replied.

As Stefanie got up to change the CD I admired her fantastic hair and I asked her how she maintained it.

'Genetics is number one but Ava Gardner once told me, "Don't bother with all these expensive hair products, honey, just go to the local drug store for *everything* – it's all just as good." For example Boots does a wonderful line of anti-frizz products by John Frieda which are cheap and amazingly good. They make a fantastic shampoo, a light cream rinse, and oil stuff which you rub on your curly or frizzy hair. I do it myself and just blow dry it,' said Stefanie.

'Well, it's beautiful hair and I love the cut, it's so modern,' I said. Then I asked her what she would take on a desert island.

'Hopefully it's a humid desert island which would make it easier on the skin and hair, because my hair would curl nicely and the skin would be moist. But it would *definitely* be sunblock,' she replied.

'Join the club,' I quipped. Then I asked if she had heroes and heroines.

'My heroes have always been achievers,' she said. 'I've admired many actors. I was very privileged to come to Hollywood on the tail end of the Star System. I began to work at 15, and when I was put under contract at Columbia, they still believed in "grooming" their young hopefuls. That process allowed me to learn how movies were made since the studio was my playground. In many ways, the experience of working with such movie greats as John Wayne,

'Life is about change and you must embrace change and commit yourself to it if you want to move forward.'

Maureen O'Hara, Bing Crosby, Van Heflin, Lee Remick, Lana Turner, Cliff Robertson, David Niven, Claudia Cardinale, helped to give me a sense of the importance of balancing life and career. However, I have two real heroines. I had the privilege of playing Beryl Markham in a movie. In 1934 she was the first person ever to fly solo, west across the Atlantic. Lindberg tried it in the late 20s and said it *could not* be done, because no plane could carry that much fuel. Beryl carried as much fuel as she could, but she crash-landed in Nova Scotia and didn't make New York as planned. She barely made it but she made it. She grew up in Kenya and I identify with that. She died in the 80s at 84. My second favourite person was the anthropologist Margaret Mead. Neither of these women ever accepted a stop sign or anything that said 'you can't do this!'. They were totally self-motivated, and acted out of a desire for adventure and pursuing their own interests. I'm sure that both of them must have encountered criticism and obstacles at some point, but this did not stop them. They were real pioneers.'

'There aren't many of those around today,' I said.

Stefanie told me that during filming she flew herself in a Gypsy Moth. 'There seems to be no end to your versatility and courage,' I said. ' I'm very impressed.'

'Well, I love it,' she said. 'I don't feel ready to slow my pace yet. I could *never* be the sort of woman who goes on vacation and sits on a beach. I'm high energy and take pleasure in doing things and I've an innate curiosity about so many things. There's a saying in Hollywood that when the make-up comes off you've still got to go home and face your life, so you better make sure it's as good as the one you left at the dressing table. Life is about change and you *must* embrace change and commit yourself to it if you want to move forward.'

'People do change, and now that we live longer it's hardly surprising that sequential monogamy is the way of choice now,' I said. 'Many people will, hopefully, live to be in their nineties. If you marry at 20 you may have outgrown them (or vice versa) by 40 – and there's still another 40 or 50 years left to share with someone else.'

'I think we have the potential not only of living longer but living in a much better physical condition,' said Stefanie. '*If* you take care of yourself.'

I asked Stefanie how many languages she speaks.

'Seven,' she said modestly. 'Polish, and Russian which is my first language, English is my second, French, Spanish, Italian, Swahili and some Mandarin Chinese. '

'I'm *so* jealous,' I sighed. 'How did you learn to speak all of them?'

'I was self-taught.'

'You must have studied like *mad*. What discipline! It's enviable.' I said. 'So basically, what is your philosophy of life?'

'My favourite saying is: "It's not the arrival that's important, it's the journey! It's the journey and not the discovery. The best process of life is the process of life *itself* and not the achievement because if the *process* is good the achievement is axiomatic, and once having *achieved* something all you look for is the *next* achievement, so if you're not in love with the process, the achievement in itself is an empty thing." For example engaging in a relationship is an art to be cultivated and enjoyed. There's a quote from the *Zen Book of Wisdom*: "If you do not get it from yourself where will you go for it?"

Stefanie Powers is a woman who is totally fulfilled yet always questing for fulfilment – truly a Renaissance woman of today. She has a resilience, a spirit for adventure and knowledge that will never be quenched. If I had to be wrecked on a desert island with anyone, then I'd choose her.

Photographed on the set of **Joan Rivers'** Tonight *show, Hollywood, 1983.*

JOAN RIVERS
CAN WE TALK?

THE FIRST TIME I appeared on Joan Rivers' prime time talk show I found her quite abrasive and absolutely terrifying. The second time I realised she was not nearly as intimidating as she portrayed herself on TV, but was in fact charming, pleasant and funny, a devoted mother whose professional stock in trade was to be as outrageous as possible.

When she asked me on her show, 'Joan, who's the best lover you've ever had?' I shot back with: 'Your husband, darling!' Joan almost fell off her chair with shock. In the commercial break she leaned forward and whispered anxiously:

'It's not *true* is it? You didn't go to bed with my Edgar?'

'Of *course* not,' I laughed. 'I was just kidding.'

'Oh, thank goodness,' she sighed, 'I couldn't have taken that.'

Joan and I have been good friends ever since. I've guested on her TV and radio shows many times and have been to wonderful dinner parties at her fabulous New York apartment.

Joan began her career in the late 50s doing stand-up in tiny nightclubs, where they would 'pass round the hat' instead of paying her. She gained a cult following and by 1960 was doing standing room only business at Chicago's renowned 'Second City'. Joan is one of the hardest working women in show business... a comedienne, author of six books, a newspaper columnist, an actress, a screen writer, a night-club headliner, a business woman and an award-winning television and radio chat-show hostess. She has also had unprecedented success with record-breaking sales of over $160 million in sales of the *Joan Rivers Classics Collection* of jewellery on QVC.

During her ascent in show business Joan has suffered defeats, humiliations and tragedy, all of which she uses brilliantly in her witty act.

She took over from Johnny Carson as host of *The Tonight Show* in the mid-eighties and was subsequently ignominiously dropped, but her popularity continued to grow and she became the highest-rated chat show hostess in the UK and US, winning an Emmy in 1990 for outstanding Talk Show Host.

The same year as starring in a TV movie with her daughter, based on their then rocky relationship, Joan was nominated for both Tony and Drama Desk Awards for her outstanding performance in a Broadway play.

She is tireless on the charity circuit, as national spokesperson for the Cystic Fibrosis Foundation and an advocate for Suicide Prevention and since 1982 has been actively involved in the fight against AIDS. Her signature phrase 'Can we talk' is so well known that it has been patented and I was looking forward to our talk as I arrived at the Ritz Hotel in London, where I met Joan for tea in her suite. It was a chilly afternoon in June but Joan was looking fabulous in a wonderful blue Armani suit, her trade mark Joan Rivers pearl jewellery, and exquisite beige stilettoes. Her hair and make-up were immaculate as usual, and she held herself beautifully, a trim 5'2' and petite size 6. I asked her about her beauty regime.

'I wish I had a real great regime,' she sighed,

'but I'm very hit or miss. I think a lot of it is genetic – basically I have very good skin, which came from my grandmother. I'm so damn busy all the time, but I always take off all my make-up and cleanse properly with dry clean towels. I *love* make-up – wouldn't go out without it. I believe in make-up *totally*. If someone shrieks "Fire", I'd reach for my eye-liner before I left the building.'

I asked her what she'd take on a desert island and without hesitation she said eye-liner. 'You can always moisturise elbows and knees with wet leaves soaked in water.'

I asked Joan for her secret to always being so well dressed and she answered, 'I only wear very plain clothes – never loud prints, stripes or dots but I like strong colours. Jewellery can make a plain dark suit or dress very adaptable. Lots of pearls or one great pin. I wear my own line of jewellery, hoping some man will say, "Let me match that for you in real gems," she joked.

I asked her how she managed to appear taller than 5'2" and she said she always wore high heels. 'I'm a fifth generation stiletto wearer. I walk two miles every day in high heels in the city – I walk *everywhere*. If I have to go to someone's office on the third floor I'll *walk* up and I'll walk *down*. Because up builds muscle, down builds bone – of course, I'll wear sneakers on the treadmill. Then I always carry my own bags when I'm travelling because then your arms get a working out too. I exercise a *lot* and I do weights three times a week. I also keep heavy rubber bands with me so when I'm not doing anything else, for instance when I'm doing my two-hour radio show, I'll use those for my arms. I'm very aware of *constantly* using my body.'

'Even when you're watching TV?' I asked.

'Joan Crawford used to sit at dinner parties with her legs raised one inch from the ground all night. That *really* works those tummy muscles – what dedication,' she said admiringly,

'Joan Crawford used to sit at dinner parties with her legs raised one inch from the ground all night'

putting sweetener into her milkless tea. 'But no one ever said beauty maintenance was easy. And past 50 it gets a lot tougher.'

'My mother always said "You have to suffer to be beautiful,"' I said.

'So did mine,' said Joan. 'Sure it gets more difficult, but I'm *amazed* at how many women I know who look *better* now than they did when they were 30 or 40. Women really try harder these days.'

I decide to ask her the $64,000 question, what did she think about plastic surgery?

'Yes! Yes! Yes! Absolutely,' she crowed. '*God* made plastic surgeons! I'm open about cosmetic surgery because practically everyone I know in this business has had it, but I haven't had nearly as much done as the media has made out. I had a full lift, my nose thinned and my eyes done years ago, and it *really* made me feel better about myself.'

'We're in a totally youth-orientated career market today,' I said. 'So if a woman over 50 needs to compete with 30-year-olds she should take advantage of what's on offer.'

'Right,' said Joan. 'And what's wrong with a little help? – a touch of lipo on the thighs, a tummy tuck or having your eye bags eradicated? Sure it's painful sometimes but so is exercise.'

I asked her how long a face lift lasts. 'I go to my surgeon every six months or so and ask if it's time for a touch up. Face it – you maintain your house and paint it every five or ten years and a good facelift should usually last about five years. It's like servicing a car – every 20,000 miles you *have* to have it done. Everyone needs a little tuck or peel here and there. Most of the women I know in New York are doing little things all the time for maintenance.'

'Like what?' I asked.

'The skin peel,' said Joan.

'I've heard such horror stories about women's skin coming off and going bright red. Isn't that dangerous?' I said.

'Yeah and so's crossing the road,' quipped Joan. 'Let's get real here. It only takes a little tuck to keep the chin looking good. One Christmas I gave all my staff cosmetic surgery of their choice... and they all took it!' She laughed. 'It's better than giving a cashmere sweater. My housekeeper chose a facelift, my manager got her nose done and Melissa's ex-governess had her thighs lipo-ed. Everyone was *real* happy,' she grinned.

I asked her whom she considered the best cosmetic surgeon in the US and she said, 'I guess Steven Hoefflin and Frank Camer are two of them, but there are many good surgeons around. A lot depends on a woman's skin and a lot on luck.'

'So basically do you believe that having cosmetic surgery can be a bit of a gamble?' I asked.

'Sure. They say that even a great race horse trips,' she smiled.

'Could a plain girl get good results from cosmetic surgery?' I asked.

'*Yes*, and she *should*. It would do *so* much

'**Any woman who chooses not to have a child has lost 70 per cent of the joy of their life.**'

for her, *and* for her ego. I've never seen a woman who's had something done who didn't feel better about herself. I say, if you have enough cash for a new car – forget the car. Take the money and get yourself a new face instead!'

'Let's face it, people have always wanted to improve their appearance. But what about wrinkles? Face lifts can't get rid of them,' I said.

'Wrinkles are the *worst* thing to get rid of – practically impossible. You *cannot* get rid of them *even* with a face lift – it's a peel or nothing. The best advice is don't allow yourself to get wrinkles in the first place. So stay out of that sun, which is what I've always done. I had a little skin cancer removed from my lip 28 years ago and the doctor said that I must *never* go in the sun again. So it was a good warning which I've heeded.'

She poured some more tea and offered me a biscuit which I took but she didn't. 'So what do you eat, Joan?' I asked.

'Very very little,' she said. 'If I even *look* at a doughnut or a piece of cake it goes straight to my hips so I eat tiny, *tiny* meals several times a day and of course no dough, no fat and *no* sugar.'

'Of course.' I guiltily put down my biscuit and our talk turned to children as Joan is exceedingly close to her daughter Melissa.

'Any woman who chooses not to have a child has lost 70% of the joy of their life,' she said. 'I have *so* many friends without children who've elected *not* to have them, but I know they'd be happier if they had.'

I asked her how she relaxed and she said, 'I'm lucky because I can turn off very easily. One day a week I do *absolutely* nothing at all. I mean *zero*. I don't get dressed. I switch off the phones and I just sit around, vegetate, read and watch TV. It's so relaxing and I feel rejuvenated the next day.'

'Every now and again I *love* being a couch potato,' I agreed. 'Even though it feels sinful.'

I moved on to what she thought about the way women dressed today.

'I think it's disgusting to go to the theatre or dinner and not look good. To not even *try* to look glamorous. Glamour has *nothing* to do with whether you're pretty or even young. It's your look – your style that makes it. Few women have it today – except us,' she laughed.

'It seems to have become a lost art,' I said. 'And considered unfashionable too – but since I enjoy looking glamorous, I'm *never* going to give up.'

'Me neither,' said Joan.

I asked her about heroes and heroines and she said immediately, 'Jackie Onassis. To have your husband's brains in your lap and to pull yourself together, get up, get out and get on with it is a triumph; to continue to raise two terrific children and to look *fabulous* – and *then* make a whole new life. *That's* my kind of heroine.'

'I agree. Jackie O has always been one of my heroines too. In the 60s she was like Princess Diana, don't you think?'

'Before JFK was killed – absolutely. She was the most glamorous woman in the world bar none,' said Joan.

'So what's your philosophy of how to get through this life?' I asked.

'Enjoy every minute and look the best you can *all* the time!'

With those words of wisdom ringing in my ears I had to leave as Joan was off to QVC to sell her jewellery. We made plans to see each other the next time I was in New York and we *Mwah Mwahed* air kisses so as not to smudge each other's make-up. Joan Rivers – feisty, funny and formidable – a self-made multi-millionairess with a hard edge, but a warm and caring friend and mother and a brilliant business woman.

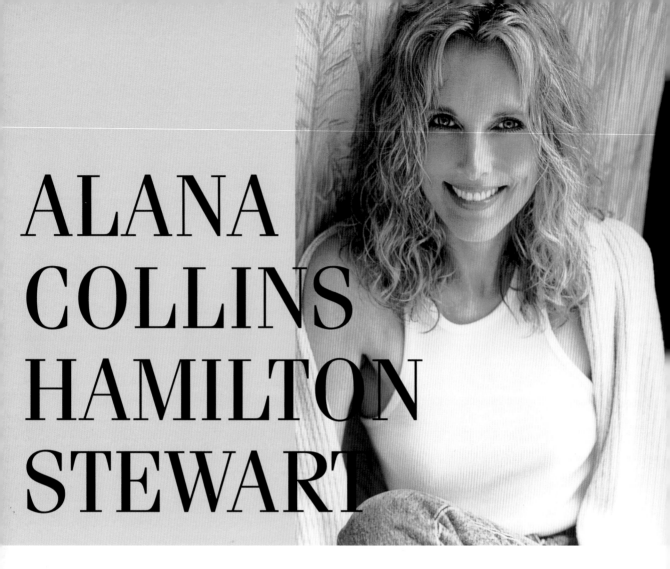

ALANA COLLINS HAMILTON STEWART

THE OTHER COLLINS GIRL

The sun had finally decided to put in a welcome appearance on the dank May afternoon I drove to Alana Stewart's house. She had just moved in and her charming ranch-style house high in the hills above Mulholland Drive in Beverly Hills was in a state of organised chaos. Workmen wandered in and out drilling, hanging pictures, pushing and pulling but Alana herself seemed quite sanguine amidst this sea of turmoil. Casually dressed in a long black cotton skirt and white shirt, her thick

blonde hair framed her pale oval face in a style that suited her perfectly. She appeared to be wearing no make-up but in the thirty years I've known Alana she's *never* looked as if she wore make-up. Even in the 60s, when everyone was plastered in it, she stood out for the simplicity of her beauty.

The first time I met her I was married to

Photographed by Eddie Sanderson at Alana's house, Beverly Hills, 14 May 1998.

Anthony Newley and Alana came to a party at our house with her date. A Ford model in New York doing commercials and small roles on TV, she was dewy-fresh, straight out of Texas and with the charming drawl to go with it.

Thirty years, three children and two husbands later the drawl is hardly noticeable but the outgoing Texan charm and bonhomie is still well in evidence.

'I was always tanned – well, hey, look who I was married to!'

Soon after her arrival in Hollywood in the mid-60s Alana Collins captured the heart of that elusive bachelor and man about Hollywood George Hamilton. Their marriage was stormy, to say the least, but I was sad when they split as they seemed totally suited to each other. They had one son, Ashley, now 25.

In the late 70s Alana married Rod Stewart, another tumultuous relationship that produced two children, Kimberley – who inherited her mother's blonde looks and is now modelling – and Sean.

The Stewarts seemed ecstatically happy in a passionately volatile relationship and divided their time between London and LA. I often saw them in the 70s and 80s at their star-studded parties. However, all good things come to an end and Alana and Rod eventually divorced.

Alana revived her acting career and was then linked to various swains, including Sylvester Stallone, but her most constant date and closest companion was her first husband George Hamilton. Recently the couple did a daily syndicated talk show, a modern day version of Gracie Allan and George Burns. Their chemistry was electric as they bantered

and bickered with each other and Alana surprised audiences with her spontaneity and sense of humour. The dynamic duo are still in demand as hosts and they remain closer friends than ever.

Alana has always been a central part of Hollywood's 'A' list party scene and at her birthday party the week of this interview, the cast included Jack Nicholson, Warren Beatty, Jackie Bisset, Allan Carr, Tina Sinatra and some of Tinseltown's top agents. It was a warm family occasion too as Kimberley and Sean dropped in later.

Now that her children have grown up, Alana is busy writing scripts, and is designing her own line of costume jewellery which she sells on the Home Shopping Channel.

I admired a fabulous orchid pin that she was wearing.

'I found the original with a vintage jewellery dealer. This is an *exact* replica and there's a cute story behind it. During World War II men couldn't buy orchids, or corsages for their girlfriends, so they started making these orchid pins, the men would buy them and give them to their girlfriends instead of the real flowers.'

'I hope the line is really successful,' I said, then asked her, 'What do you do first thing in the morning to your skin?'

'I don't wear a lot of make-up because (a), it's bad for your skin in my opinion and (b), I find a lot of make-up ages you. When women get to 35 or 40 they should greatly reduce the make-up.'

'So what do you do to protect your skin from the elements then?'

'I believe it's hereditary, luck really. A lot of it has to do with genes; my grandmother had fabulous skin, and so did my mother, and I inherited it.'

'But you must have a skin care routine because I remember you telling me about it.'

'Well, I use a really gentle cleanser because

I have extremely sensitive skin, it's too sensitive for all those new glycolic acids, fruit acids, all these wonderful things that are supposed to exfoliate. After the cleanser I put on a really good night cream before going to bed and I use eye cream *religiously*. I've been using it since I was 19. I put on any brand I happen to like at the given moment – I move between Sisley and La Prairie. It's crucially important to use eye cream for preventing lines. Moisturiser's essential, too. I used to sleep with a humidifier in my room all the time, because out here it's too dry, and dryness is the worst thing for the complexion. Think of a piece of leather, like a saddle or a purse – if you don't use leather softeners or something to keep it moisturised, it cracks. I think our skin is the same. I was a fanatical sun-worshipper until I turned 38 and then I stopped. I was always tanned – well, hey,

look who I was married to! We spent half our lives tanning!'

We laughed and I asked Alana to tell me her basic philosophy of life.

'You have to be positive and not allow yourself to think about negative, bad things. All that ties in with beauty and what's inside always shows on the outside. Sometimes you see women who may be young but somehow they look old, tired, angry and bitter. And then you see other women who are older, and yet they have a glow, a life force that really shines through. Like you, for instance!'

'And like you, for instance!' I said as Alana continued:

'I believe what's inside you *really* comes out on your face. Your face reflects the way you think about life, your perspective on life. I believe a lot of how you look depends on how

Photographed at a Hollywood party, with Tom Selleck, 1983.

you treat others, because in the end *everything* comes back to you. You must try to be kind and respectful and considerate.'

'Yes,' I agreed. 'Your face reflects the true state of your body's physical, emotional and mental condition. Now, you've got a really great body, you're enviably slim and you have three children. So what's your exercise routine?'

'Very little. I'm naturally thin, and I'm always trying to gain weight, which makes most people want to strangle me. When I was a kid I ate like a truck driver, and I looked like a tall, skinny reed – it was a joke among my family and friends. I'm still trying to gain weight.'

'Women will *hate* you, Alana. You must do *some* exercise.'

'I do yoga, and a little bit of Chi Gong, but I do very little other exercise. I walk every day because that is important. Sometimes, if I'm really busy, I'll try to walk five or ten minutes on the treadmill. I do a little bit of aerobics and I occasionally do weights. If I'm watching television I'll do my 8 pound weights for my arms and my biceps.'

'*Eight* pounds? That's quite heavy.'

'Oh, I can use up to 18 pounds. I'm strong.'

I felt Alana's beautifully toned arm. 'You certainly are – and you've got *perfect* muscle definition.'

'I *religiously* do arm exercises. I do an isometric exercise every other day, just to keep the back of the arm firm because I think there's nothing worse than flabby arms.'

'"Kimono arms"'. The curse of the over-forties. Tell me about this isometric exercise?'

Alana stood with her arms out, her knees a little bent, then turned her arms and palms behind her back, and tensed them.

'That's all?' I said.

'Yes, but I do it a hundred times. Can you feel how it tightens the back of your arms? That's all I do for the back of my arms, except arm-curls for the biceps and a few raisers for the shoulders when I'm watching TV. When I'm washing my face I'll do leg lifts on the spot.'

'You do have a fabulous butt,' I commented and Alana laughed.

'It used to be better, my dear. It's hanging down a lot lower than it should be.'

'It doesn't look like that to me. So what else do you do to get such a tight butt?'

'Leg lifts while I'm brushing my teeth. I try to do them two or three times a week, fifteen on each side.'

'So basically, you use the time when you're doing other things to do exercises that can improve your body – that's brilliant!'

'Yes, I have to do something; otherwise I get bored. My mind's all over the place, so I can talk on the phone, read a magazine, listen to the stereo, do my nails, exercise, brush my teeth, do *something* that's constructive.'

'Typical Gemini,' I said. 'You've got incredibly strong white teeth. You always clean them three times a day, right?'

'I brush them a lot. I didn't go to a dentist till I was almost 30. I don't think I had my teeth cleaned till then. I was raised in Texas on well-water and never had a cavity.'

'Lucky you. But your teeth are *so* white, they're absolutely perfect, and I know you've not had them capped. Do you brush your gums as well? My dentist says you *must* brush the gums, otherwise they'll shrink.'

'I use dental floss every day. My dentist told me I had to do that religiously, so I do, *and* I brush my teeth after every time I eat.'

'You don't think that could take the enamel off?'

'Well, it hasn't yet,' she laughed. 'And I haven't got many years left... Face it, by now I've probably lived more years than I'm going to live, unless I'm going to be really geriatric.'

'I've read that Cher is in a complete state about being in her fifties. How do *you* feel about ageing?' I asked.

'I think it's better than the alternative. I'd like not to age, but the alternative is to die, and I'd prefer not to do that yet as I'm leading a very full life now. Twenty years ago I thought 50 was *death*, that there was nothing else but sit down in your rocking chair, with the cat, and hope your kids came to visit occasionally. Now I find this is one of the most productive times in my life,' she said.

'Don't you believe, as I do, that there's a whole generation of 40- to 75-year-olds who are extremely productive?'

'Yes, but our whole culture is much too focused on youth,' said Alana. 'Too many women over 35 start to feel like used-up has-beens because that's the way society looks at them. A number of us are changing that attitude towards older women. Whatever you see yourself as, you become, and I don't see myself as anything but youthful, and ageing gracefully. I've never had plastic surgery. I look at my neck sometimes and I think hmm maybe – but I'm too terrified. I've seen pictures of what they do, and it's scary, so right now I just

'I'd like not to age, but the alternative is to die, and I'd prefer not to do that yet.'

prefer to *think* young. I believe that if you think of yourself as ageless you will be."

'That is *exactly* what I believe,' I said. 'Age is a number and mine's unlisted.'

'What does it *matter* if you're 40, 50 or 60?' said Alana. 'It *doesn't*. It's how you *look*, and *feel* and *think*. People are too caught up with age. In practically every culture in the world except America and Britain older people are revered and respected. Here it's *all* about youth, especially in the entertainment industry. Getting older is *very* difficult for a woman in this business. Think about all the women in the world in their fifties and sixties who need to be inspired, who need to be told that they're not over the hill, that their best years are *not* over, that they *can* still be productive. It's up to women like us, who have these kind of lives, to be *their* inspirations.'

'Well you certainly are, Alana.' A workman walked through and started drilling, so we went into Alana's large marble bathroom, where she leaned over the vanity and started brushing her hair.

'You've got such fabulous hair,' I said. 'It always looks good and I like the new shorter cut. Do you have any tricks for making it look *better*?'

'I decided to be more *au courant*,' she grimed. 'Long blonde hair is a little dated, too kind of 70s and 80s. Today it's younger and fresher to have shorter hair. Again, my hair is obviously genetic.'

'It's not fair! You've had a *really* great set of genetics. Hair, skin, teeth and no weight problems!'

'But I'm also flat-chested and I've got thick calves. You don't get everything.'

'*Nobody* gets everything,' I said. 'Nobody. So, you're not into dieting *per se*, but I know that there are many things that you won't eat.'

'I eat very healthily, but I have lots of food allergies. I don't eat dairy or much fat, mostly because I have sensitive digestion. I try to avoid anything fried, spicy or oily.'

'So you don't eat junk?'

'Oh, if I could I would. My favourite meal is a Johnny Rocket's hamburger, milk shake and chilli fries.'

'You can really eat that and look like this?' I asked in amazement.

'At least once a month I have to have a big juicy hamburger and chocolate milk shake.'

'I've always believed a little of what you fancy does you good, so once a month's not bad.'

'And I *love* chocolate. I'm not a champagne and caviar person. I'd much prefer a hamburger and shake.'

'Do you drink wine?' I asked.

'I wish I could, but it doesn't make me feel good. I had Epstein-Barr some time ago, which affects your liver, so since then I've not been able to really drink. I might occasionally have an aperitif.'

I asked Alana what her daily diet consisted of and she said, 'For breakfast I eat porridge, or occasionally rice cereal, cream of wheat, hot cereal and toast, and then sometimes I'll have a weight-gain drink mid-morning.'

'You're going to get hate mail,' I joked, and Alana gave a peal of laughter.

'It's *not* easy gaining weight,' she protested. 'So I usually eat sandwiches for lunch – a turkey or a tuna fish sandwich. I eat a lot of them as I need the bread to gain weight. I don't go out to lunch because I find it a waste of time. I have a snack every afternoon – crackers or tuna fish. I've also got a passion for cookies and scones *and* muffins and I always eat a proper dinner every night.'

'Do you usually go out for dinner?'

'I don't go out much at all.'

I laughed. 'Alana, you *always* say that, and then I see you *everywhere*.'

'It's not true,' she laughed with me. 'I hardly ever go out. Last night I went to a little

Italian restaurant with Kimberley but I hardly ever go to dinner with friends. I've only been to the new Spago once since it opened, and I haven't been to Mortons in two years, except for the *Vanity Fair* Oscars party – which is probably the only big dressy event I've been to in months.'

'So do you just like to chill out?'

'Yes, I lead a boring life. I stay home, alone most of the time. There's so much to do in a day and so much to deal with mentally; the kids, the jewellery line, the house, my business, and all the other things that one has to deal with on a daily basis – by the end of the day I'm so tired. I usually eat dinner in the kitchen. I have a wonderful housekeeper and I like to cook too. Sometimes I'll make a huge lasagne and eat nothing but lasagne and garlic bread for three days. I love pasta – and I like desserts. I have a real sweet tooth.'

'So, darling, eating sounds like a full-time job for you. How do you turn off?'

'I never miss my morning ten minutes of yoga or Chi Gong, which is an energy workout, and then I meditate for about twenty minutes or read some inspirational literature to get my mind in the right direction. Around 5.30 I'll do a little more yoga, sometimes just ten minutes, and deep breathing, then I meditate again, and do a deep relaxation exercise, a guided relaxation on tape. That really de-stresses me more than anything and it's what keeps me going. Ever since I had the Epstein-Barr virus I seem to get tired and I have to rest at the end of the day. I sleep eight hours every night and I think that is another reason why I look as good as I do. I've slept eight hours every night of my life. Sometimes, if I have to wake up early, it's only seven hours, but *never* less than that because while you're sleeping that's when your body repairs itself.'

'So what would you take on a desert island to beautify yourself if you could only take one

thing?' I asked.

'I'd take my moisturiser.'

'That's everybody's favourite,' I said. 'Who are your heroes and heroines?'

'I greatly admire Mother Teresa, because she was such a selfless individual.'

'Now the $64,000 question, Alana. How do you feel about love? I know you haven't been living with anyone for a while. Do you think that you ever will again?'

'I'd really love to have someone in my life, but I would want it to be different this time. I'm so much more settled now than when I was in my twenties and thirties. I don't want drama and excitement. I don't want fights anymore. I want serenity and happiness and mutual support. In this business you have to go out occasionally, but I really like living a very quiet private life. Serenity is very important to me now. I'm not saying I don't want to travel or have a good time, but I couldn't *bear* to be married to a wealthy power mogul, live in a big city and go out to charity functions or dinners every night. I'd rather *die.*'

'I can't imagine anything more stressful, but I know many women who do that. Constantly having to get done up and find a new dress and chat to boring people all night,' I said.

'To me that would be a fate worse than death,' said Alana. 'I mean, I go *days* without putting on make-up.'

'So what's next for you Alana?' I asked.

'I'm continuing my jewellery collection for Home Shopping and QVC in England,' she said. 'And I've just finished filming a movie with Timothy Leary. I put my career on hold when I had children. I always had creative ambitions, but I wasn't able to fulfil them while raising my children. I don't think people should have kids unless they're willing to make them a priority.'

'You were and are a great mother,' I said. 'I know when they were growing up you devoted

'I'd really love to have someone in my life, but I would want it to be different this time. Serenity is very important to me.'

your every waking moment to them.'

'That's why although I wanted to work, I couldn't,' she said. 'The kids were and are number one in my life.'

With that she went to the stereo, put on a CD, and thumping New Wave sounds poured out. 'That's Ashley. His first recording,' she said proudly. 'You've got to move on. My career remains a work in progress. What most people don't know is that I grew up dirt poor in a tiny house out in the country with no indoor plumbing. Boy, would I love to play a character like that! So that's why I'm writing and creating roles for myself to play – 'cause you've got to

make your own breaks.'

Suddenly a workman started to drill the walls so violently that we had to move into the sitting room. Eddie started taking our photographs as we gossiped about the guests at her birthday party.

I adore Alana, who's one of my best friends in LA. Although she has to be careful to get enough rest and relaxation, having suffered from the debilitating ME, she's still a ton of fun and now that her children are grown she is determined to create a whole new persona for herself – and I believe she will succeed.

BARBARA TAYLOR BRADFORD

A TRUE WOMAN OF SUBSTANCE

Barbara Taylor Bradford was looking wonderfully spring-like when we met for lunch in the Dorchester's Grill Room in May. Her pale beige linen suit with a tangerine silk lining, matching blouse, Rene Mancini linen shoes and a coral flower pin and earrings from Van Cleef & Appels – 'Another present from Bob,' she smiled, was extremely chic. One of Britain's best selling and wealthiest popular novelists, her success increases with each book. Barbara looks much younger than her age and she was positively bursting with excitement at being in London for the publication of her new book, *The General*.

Born in Yorkshire in the 30s Barbara was a journalist on the *Yorkshire Evening Post, Woman's Own* and *London Evening News* before she started writing. Her first novel, *A Woman of Substance*, was published in 1979. That enduring best-seller was followed by twelve others, of which ten have been made into television mini-series. Her novels have sold more than fifty-six million copies worldwide in more than eighty-eight countries and have been translated into thirty-eight languages. Barbara lives in New York City and Connecticut with her film producer husband Robert Bradford.

'We met in London in the 60s,' she smiles. 'It was a blind date, but it was love at first sight.'

They married eighteen months later, settled in New York and thirty-three years later they are as close as ever; and their marriage has become a well-marked partnership of two strong personalities. 'We are both workaholics and unrepentant romantics,' Barbara states.

Each of her novels has been dedicated to

'Bob', who in turn marks each new volume by surprising the author with a fabulous piece of jewellery.

As we are both fond of our food we chose asparagus vinaigrette to start with followed by grilled Dover sole. I ordered creamed spinach, but Barbara requested chips. 'I love chips,' she confessed. Barbara had a glass of champagne, I a kir.

'You have wonderful skin, Barbara. It's so clear and pale and I'd love to know your beauty routine,' I said.

'Most beauty experts would frown on it. I use Elizabeth Arden milky cleanser at night and then I rinse my face in warm water. Everybody says *don't* put water on your face but I do. Then I take it off with tissues or a face cloth or just my hands. I use different products at times, because I think your skin gets used to things, and I put moisturiser on in the morning... When I'm working, I go to my desk with just moisturiser on and sometimes at night I rub in one of those miracle creams that are supposed to regenerate the skin.'

'I asked her views on make-up and she answered, 'Oh I *love* make-up. I use liquid foundation and powder and blush – and eye-liner like you. I like the lot and it's flattering, of course. Make-up enhances everybody. I don't get this bare-faced grunge style or whatever the hell it's called.'

'Most of the women I've interviewed do care about the way they present themselves,' I said. 'Every time I've seen you you're always perfectly turned out. You're one of the few women who looks *great* at airports.'

'I always try to look nice. Thank you.'

I asked Barbara how she felt about getting older. 'I don't worry about things like that. I don't look my age and neither do you. But I don't go around *telling* people how old I am; it's the bloody papers that say she's 50-some-thing or 60-something. I always say I'm 45,

you've made a horrible mistake... I like to put them on,' she laughed.

'So you believe you're as old as you feel?' I asked.

'Yes, absolutely and I have *lots* of energy. When Gail Sheehy, the writer, did her book *Silent Passage* about menopause, she asked me, "How did you feel about the menopause?" I said, "I never had it," and she said, "What do you mean you never had it?" and I said, "I didn't have *time* to have it because I'm always so busy." I did have horrible hot flushes, they were dreadful, but I've forgotten all about them and I really don't think that I had any other symptoms. Then Gail said, "You're extremely energetic, you have what Margaret Mead, the anthropologist, called 'post-menopausal zest".' You see, Mead went all over the world studying women after menopause. Some women were wimpy, droopy and lost their reason, then there was another kind of woman who was filled with zest. I bury people with my energy.'

'Yes, the Zest Generation, that's a great epi-thet,' I said.

Our food arrived and as we dug in I asked Barbara if she thought that energy and doing things you adore keeps you young.

'Absolutely, I got such a surge of adrenalin last week. I was running about promoting my book and my play, *Dangerous to Know*, that just opened.'

'You seem to have what is called "rude good health" do you not?' I said. 'Do you believe that also comes from your attitude to life?'

'It's *all* attitude. People who say "I'm going to lick this illness" tend to get better. Let's face it, good English stock wins out. I try to be care-ful. I don't smoke, but I like a glass of cham-pagne or wine occasionally.'

I asked her about her diet and she said, 'Oh I *try*, but I'm still carrying a lot of liquid. When I finish a book it takes about a month to go. You can go somewhere to lose weight and you can go on a diet, but then you put it back on immediately. For me the secret is to try and eat *very* carefully all the time. I have my own diet. It's hard to remember ten calories here and a hundred calories there – you can't go around with a bit of paper, so what I'll say is I won't eat anything white for a while. Potatoes, bread, parsnips, rice, spaghetti. Chicken and white fish is all right and you can eat the white of an egg,' she said.

'It's impossible for a grown woman in today's affluent society to look like a stick-insect.'

'One of the great things about you, Barbara, is that you're happy with the fact that you're not as thin as a *Vogue* cover girl. So many women are aspiring to that unnatural look. It's sad.'

'It's impossible for a grown woman in today's affluent society to look like a stick-insect. I eat what I like – I don't *want* to look like Kate Moss. I would look ridiculous.'

'Is there anything that you won't eat?' I asked.

'I sometimes have an old fashioned Coke. I don't like Diet Coke. I'll have a hamburger very *occasionally*, with french fries which I love and I like veal and roast beef. For the most part I like everything but I don't always eat it all. I take vitamin C with rosehip and B6. I think that if you take vitamins every day all year you get used to them. So I just take them for a few months, then stop,' she said.

'Do you take Flame?' I asked. 'It's the calcium supplement that Barbara Cartland

highly recommends. She is *extraordinary* for ninety-odd, even though her *maquillage* leaves much to be desired,' I laughed. 'She says everyone over 50 should take it for strong bones.'

'I'll try it,' said Barbara.

I then asked Barbara if she believed in the power of positive thinking.

'Of *course*, it makes a *huge* difference. My glass is always half full, it's *never* half empty. I'm optimistic about everything; today might be bad but tomorrow's going to be better, and if it's not I'll do something to *make* it better,' she said emphatically.

'Is that how you've become so astonishingly successful?'

'Yes. Drive, ambition, dedication, hard work and talent,' she smiled. 'Not bad for a girl from Leeds! No one ever got *anywhere* sitting around just hoping. I work fourteen-hour days even now.'

'You obviously like women, as I do. Do you have many women friends?' I asked.

'Yes, lots. I'm always a bit suspicious of women who don't, aren't you?' she asked.

'It's so important. It's our sisterhood,' I said. 'And who are your heroines? Your heroines both in life and in your books are usually women of great power.'

'I love Catherine the Great, Elizabeth Tudor and Madame Curie – women who do things and are achievers. My New York masseuse has been massaging this 90-year-old little old lady on Sutton Place who's the daughter of Madame Curie. My heroines have *always* been powerful women. Why would anyone like a wimp?' she laughed. 'Yes, the heroines in my books are powerful and tough, but that doesn't mean they're hard-bitten. There's a lot of me in my books. Tough means resilient, with the power to bounce back, hard means hard-bitten, without any emotions or feelings. Another heroine of mine is Margaret Thatcher.'

'I admired her tremendously,' I said. 'Although she certainly fits into the tough and hard bitten category.'

'And I also admired Grace Kelly and I adored Ava Gardner, because she was lusty and a wonderful broad.'

'I thought Ava Gardner was the sexiest woman on the screen. You have a Grace Kelly look about you, with your fair hair and blue eyes,' I said. She seemed pleased.

I asked Barbara the desert island question and she answered, 'Mascara because I'm so pale.'

'And what's your philosophy of life?'

'Part of my philosophy is work. I'm always surprised when people say why do you work so hard? Well I do it because I *want* to and because being a writer is what I am, it's part of me. If you took my work away there would be something missing from Barbara Taylor Bradford. I also try to be a good person, and have a lot of integrity. I like to help others if I can, in a small way, by giving to charity. I try and lead a decent life as best I can, to keep working and not be jaded... my mother always said people who are bored are boring,' she said.

'My mother said that to *me* and I used to say that to *my* children,' I laughed.

'I don't like bored jaded people who don't get a kick out of things. I don't think life's a dress rehearsal. I want to enjoy it.'

I asked her about her thick, beautifully groomed hair.

'My hair is tinted, obviously, and it's not that thick, but I put rollers in this morning, which I don't often do. I tease it a bit and then spray it.'

'What do you do when you feel stressed?' I asked.

'I seldom allow myself to get stressed. Once I've thought something through I can let it go,' she answered.

'It's an art to do that,' I said. 'What about exercise?'

'I have a trainer twice a week at noon. I'm at

'Drive, ambition, dedication, hard work and talent... No one ever got anywhere sitting around hoping. I work fourteen hour days even now.'

my desk all morning so then I exercise and eat lightly at lunch time. I walk a lot in the country and our house in Connecticut has lots of stairs, which are great exercise.'

'I always walk up stairs. Do you do floor exercises?' I asked.

'Only when my trainer's there to make me,' she laughed.

I said, 'But it's *essential* to stretch.'

'I don't care *what* people think of me. I don't need them to tell me how to lead my life. If I'd listened to others I'd still be in Leeds, a grandmother pushing a grandchild in a pram, so what the world thinks doesn't really worry me. If people say "She dyes her hair," so what?'

'You enjoy health farms, don't you?'

'I'm going with Bob to La Prairie in Montreux. I went two years ago, and I *really* felt the benefit of their shots, which are made out of the embryo of a ewe. Doctor Niehaus started the clinic in the 30s. Margaret Thatcher went and so did Churchill and Adenaur. What I like about it is that when you arrive they give you the best medical check up, heart, lungs, they do a sonogram of the stomach, cancer tests, gynaecological and dental if you want. They insist that you have the check up before you get the three shots. When you get the shots it's just like having an immunisation in your bottom or your thigh. They do three over two days, and the rest of the time you can go on a diet. I go on a 1,200 calorie diet, which is prepared by a fantastic French chef so the food doesn't taste like diet food. I *always* lose weight. I don't drink, but I have the facials and manicures, pedicures, waxing and massage that I normally never have time for, and I look ten years younger when I leave,' she smiled.

'What exactly is in those shots?'

'Who knows? The shots don't make you *look* younger but they are meant to reinforce your immune system and help with the regeneration of cells. As well as that, it's an opportu-nity to enjoy a week's rest and look wonderful at the end.'

'Don't you think that our generation of women are the healthiest generation today because when we were growing up we didn't eat huge amounts of food?'

'Yes,' said Barbara. 'I remember that chocolate, butter, eggs, cheese and sugar were treats and you were very lucky – and bloody grateful, too – to get any!'

'It's now been proven that people who eat moderately live much longer and suffer less illnesses,' I said. 'The generation that was born between 1930 and 1950 has a far better chance of a healthy long life than those born in the 70s and 80s, so many of whom are *overweight* and often have serious health problems.'

Barbara agreed, and I asked her what she thought about the current mode of dressing.

'I *hate* to see people looking scruffy. I don't like unshaven men with stubble, it makes your face sore if you're kissing. I think if you're in the public eye it's important to be well-dressed, well turned out and put together. It takes a bit of effort but it's worth it, I feel. One can get ready really quickly, can't one?' she asked.

'Yes, it's much easier for me to throw on a suit and a shirt than to try to be casual,' I said.

'I'm the same. This morning it took me fifteen minutes to do my make-up and hair and get dressed. If I have to go casual I have to think, well, what am I going to wear. This is almost as casual as I get. But that's the way we were brought up, don't you think?' she asked.

'Dressing well is the best revenge,' I grinned.

We finished lunch and Barbara had to go up to her suite for another interview. As I strolled out into the soft May sunshine I thought Barbara is not only talented and glamorous but warm and incredibly down to earth. The original 'Woman of Substance' who goes from strength to strength.

Ivana Trump's New York town house in the east 60s is glamorously decorated; lush red and gold Chinese silk paper and nineteenth-century paintings cover the walls. The carpets are thick and red, and the ornate cornices above the gold and white ceilings are picked out in cream.

A successful businesswoman, entrepreneur, designer, philanthropist, athlete and mother, Ivana, a fine example of 1990s Renaissance Woman, has also written two novels and an inspirational book, *The Best Is Yet To Come.*

Ivana emigrated to Canada in 1972 after gaining a degree in physical education, became a member of the National Czech Republic ski team and worked as a fashion model. After catching the eye of mini-mogul Donald Trump, they married and Ivana moved to New York. They had three children; one of whom, Ivanka, is now a fashion model herself.

The first time I met Ivana was at her then

IVANA TRUMP

BLOWING HER OWN TRUMPETTE

husband's Trump Tower when I was promoting my scent, Spectacular. I thought that Ivana was adorable and bubbly. Whenever the press asked her what her favourite scent was she cooed, 'Oh, Spectacular of course!'

Ivana and Donald split in 1990 and after she dusted herself off with a major make-over both mentally and physically, she became a powerhouse. She served as President of the Plaza Hotel where she was honoured as 'Hotelier of the Year', became CEO of Trump's Castle Hotel and Casino, then founded her latest venture, 'The House of Ivana'.

Married again briefly to an Italian businessman, she is now dating another Italian, Count Roffredo Gaettani.

We settled down on the red plush sofa of her glitzy drawing room, sipping designer water. Ivana was looking fabulous in a lavender Thierry Mugler tight-waisted suit, the short skirt revealing her superb legs. She still flaunts her signature golden beehive hair-do which only she and Patsy from *Absolutely Fabulous* can carry off. Ivana's accent is tinged with her Czechoslovakian roots, but like many Europeans she speaks so fast it's hard to keep up with her.

I asked her if she used her own House of Ivana products.

'Of course,' she smiled. 'My regime is quite easy. I use my day cream and scrub and mask and have a facial once a month. Basically you and I don't spend as much time on grooming as people *think* we do. Like a car goes in for servicing, I have maintenance, hair, make-up,

'It's not just make-up, it's how you look at life; "it's like, hey, here I am and I'm sexy".'

pedicure, manicure. Our secret is that we do it so often we eventually become self-efficient, we do our own hair and own make-up if we have to. I know you don't have hairdressers and make-up artists following your every step and I can put myself together in half an hour and look great. It's as simple as that.'

'Most women don't realise *how* simple it is,' I said. 'Throwing on a base takes me less than a minute – no wonder they call it slap!' I told Ivana she looked fantastic, considering she'd just finished a series of business meetings and asked her about her distinctive hairstyle.

'Once my hair is set from the day before, so it's not too fluffy, I can get it together in no time,' she said. 'I put in hot rollers, put my head down, brush it, tease it a bit, push it into place. But I'm lucky, I've got very thick hair.'

'Do you believe that make-up is a skin protector?' I asked.

'Some women don't want to use make-up, they don't want to take care of themselves and they don't have plastic surgery – they want to read a book instead, that's okay with me. I want to look the best for my age so I think make-up is *essential* and I know make-up actually protects you. In my own skin care line I know *exactly* what's in the different creams. I try to do what is *best* for my skin and battling age. I don't want to pretend to be a youngster, but I do try to do the best for me. I say I'm 49 but I like to look the *best* 49. And make-up helps you. If any girl says they look better without make-up they're just fooling themselves.'

'I agree. I'm amazed that so many women don't wear make-up, and are prepared to let the elements do their damnedest.'

'Women who don't take care of themselves look like old ladies by our age. I know a 64-year-old woman who looks *unbelievable* and she's *always* worn make-up. But it's not just make-up, it's how you look at life, how you

proceed; it's like, "hey, here I am and I'm sexy". Forty-nine? What are you talking about? I don't even *think* about age. I look great, with a fabulous figure, I'm desirable, I look fantastic; it's more in your head than anything.'

I told her that she had started with the advantage of being tall and having a great face and figure.

'Lots of girls started by being tall and having a great face and body but they've let themselves go by forty. It's called discipline and you *have* to maintain it. I strongly believe in discipline.'

'Most young girls today don't have the discipline that women over 40 have,' I said.

'Which is why they'll probably end up fat, unattractive and blotchy skinned. I see many models now of Ivanka's age, 16 to 20, and they're beautiful but there's something missing. They don't eat and they don't exercise so there's no muscle. They don't do anything.

They're as skinny as can be, but even at 20 their muscles are starting to hang. These skinny girls have no proportion, and no outline. It's a disaster because in ten years they're going to look awful,' she insisted.

'It's incredible that so many models don't believe in exercise. To me, exercise is a way of life, don't you think?' I said.

'Let me tell you how I exercise. I have three trainers; one comes at six o'clock in the morning on Monday. We go on the floor to do tummy, thighs and waist. I have to start early because of my business. Now, if somebody wakes me up at 5.30 a.m. and breaks my back with exercise and costs me a lot of money he might as well be good looking, right – and mine's gorgeous.' We both laughed. 'That lasts about an hour and I do sit-ups, push-ups, you name it. On Tuesdays I have another trainer and we go jogging in Central Park.'

'I'm amazed a crowd doesn't gather,' I said.

'Then I come back and I finish the last fifteen minutes on the floor for the tummy. Thursday another guy comes, a boxer, and we do a bit of boxing and power kicking. It's unbelievable for the heartbeat, incredible for the strength of your arms, and it's great for stress relief. I exercise every day if I'm in New York. When I travel, my exercise is a hundred metre dash through Gate 78 in high heels and I don't do any sports I can't do on high heels, honey!' she laughed.

'I'm exhausted listening to you.'

One of Ivana's endearing qualities is her ability to laugh at herself. I asked her how she balanced her stressful life and how she relaxed.

'I don't think about stress. I know it's there all the time but if I *thought* about it I'd go crazy. I relax by my number one sport, skiing. In the winter skiing in the mountains and in the summer I have a hundred and ten footer, and I spend July and August floating. I water ski, I scuba dive, and do underwater photography.

'Even on the weekends I work. I get up at 7.30 or 8 a.m., there's some kind of time clock in me, there's no way I can sleep till 11 a.m. I love to garden so I work in the greenhouse or in the orchid garden. Basically to relax it's either sports or gardening. I go to the museums or art galleries. I can do a million things, but to just sit at home and slob around, no way. '

I asked her what she'd take on a desert island.

'Definitely moisturiser. I can't live without it,' she replied.

'You look like somebody who hardly eats, but I'm sure you do. With your energy you must have a good appetite. Tell me your diet secrets.'

'When I finish exercising I have coffee and a protein drink because the muscles need nourishment. If you don't nourish them then

Photographed by Julio Donoso as Ivana models at the Thierry Mugler show, 17 October 1991.

'Women want to be loved and hugged, kissed, admired and cherished and it's what we search for, but do we always get it?'

the muscles are *not* going to grow. I have a yoghurt in the morning, or three or four hard boiled eggs, but *only* the white not the yolk. Whites are full of protein and they fill you up, yellow is a horror story of cholesterol. Then I never eat lunch, I don't have time. If I get hungry I'll eat another four egg whites.'

'I thought that too many eggs were bad for you,' I said in surprise, finding the idea of eating just one boiled egg white, let alone six, quite unpleasant.

'I can eat up to a dozen eggs a day but *only* the white. All the trainers eat hard boiled eggs. One egg white is only 20 calories. I don't eat aeroplane food, I take six hard boiled eggs with me. When I arrive at the hotel I call room service for a dozen hard boiled eggs and, I must say, the request is usually greeted with surprise. They have no idea what in the hell I'm doing with those eggs,' she grinned.

'You don't eat fruit or vegetables?' I asked.

'I don't. When I go out at night I celebrate with a great salad or asparagus then chicken, fish or steak... I hate rice, so a potato here and there is okay. I have greens, steak once a month and I hate sweets, which is good news. I get a pimple if I eat just one chocolate... and you know what they say about cheese, it goes *right* on your hips. But, I admit, I cannot be without champagne and wine. My grandma had a vineyard where I'd go during the war. After the war we didn't have Coca-Cola, or orange juice, and I didn't see a banana until I was aged 12.'

'Neither did I,' I said.

'Give me two bottles of wine and I'm okay,' laughed Ivana.

'You know that if you just eat *one* particular food for three days, whether it's eggs, peaches or chocolate, you'll lose weight,' I said, then asked her if she had any heroines.

'I admired Margaret Thatcher, she was fabulous. But I really never looked up to people, I did what I felt was right for me and I never copied anybody. I tried to be an original – I followed my own instincts and never idolised anyone else,' she said proudly.

'Ivana, you are *absolutely* your own person and totally unique,' I then asked her the $64,000 dollar question: 'How important is love and sex to you?'

'It's definitely important for every woman. This is what we're all about. We want to be loved and hugged, kissed, admired and cherished and it's what we search for, but do we always get it? Sometimes we do, sometimes we don't, sometimes we *think* that we have it and we don't. Women like to be desirable and attractive to the opposite sex, it's why we dress for them and try to look our best,' she said earnestly.

'It's interesting you say that, Ivana, because I know many women between 40 and 60 who *don't* have a man in their lives, but say "Oh I'm perfectly happy this way". But I wonder whether they really *are* because, like you, I enjoy sharing my life – as long as it's with the right man. I've kissed a lot of frogs but I've found my prince.' Ivana nodded vigorously.

'Honey, I broke up with Donald eight years ago. It took me a year to shake everything off, and pick myself up, but it taught me how to *survive*.'

'You are a tremendous role model for women, Ivana. I know *many* women who admire you because of how you stood up for yourself in your divorce with Donald. You didn't let it destroy you in any way, in fact it made you stronger. There's that saying 'that which does not kill you makes you stronger'. Do you think it's true of you?' I asked.

She laughed: 'As devastating as it was, I had no *idea* how many opportunities would open for me after my divorce. There was a whole new world. If I hadn't divorced Donald I would still be running his hotels and his casinos and catering to him. I didn't want to do that anymore because Donald always said, "I taught

'If I hadn't divorced Donald I would still be running his hotels and his casinos and catering to him.'

you everything", so I refused to give him that satisfaction any longer. He always took the credit for *anything* I did if it was associated with the business I was doing with him. He'd say, "I gave you great advice and now you're using it to make big bucks. It's all because of me". So I just dumped all his stuff and went into books, fashion, cosmetics, because Donald cannot claim he taught me that! Now I have two companies. One of them is the House of Ivana, which produces a line of clothes, jewellery, cosmetics and accessories and we are on television around the world. I manufacture *all* my merchandise, skin care and clothes. I'm not just a celebrity, I design the stuff, I have my own factory, I do everything.'

'So you are totally self-made,' I said.

'I'm a vendor,' she said proudly.

'And brilliant at it,' I said. 'How many languages do you speak, Ivana?'

'I speak English, then all Eastern European languages, Czech, Russian, Polish, Hungarian, German, but lousy Italian and French.'

'I bet it's not so lousy – my God, that's eight languages.'

Ivana then told me about the hotel she was restoring in Zagreb with suites to be called 'The Ivana Suites', the casino she will open in Dubrovnik, her forthcoming advice book for women and the magazine she was launching, like *Martha Stewart's Living* called *Ivana's World*.

'I *must* have control,' she said firmly. 'It's essential to me.'

'You're obviously a workaholic,' I said.

'Honey – you said it,' she laughed. 'And I love it. C'mon, time to work, let's do these pictures.'

When I left Ivana's town house it was with a sense that I'd just spent an hour with a woman of extraordinary achievement. She has probably accomplished more businesswise than any single woman that I can think of. She is also enormously charming, funny and feminine. She had given me a stylish black satin bag filled with her products packaged in pink, black and gold; eau de toilette Ivana, fragrance Ivana, bubbling bath oil Ivana, Ivana eye shadows, Ivana body shampoo – a veritable cornucopia of Ivana goodies.

Later that night I dined with Ivana and her boyfriend Roffredo at an Italian restaurant.

I observed that Ivana ate what she said she did, just salad and meat. We also hit the wine, but what *did* surprise me was that she smoked three cigarettes.

'If I feel like one occasionally, why not?' she shrugged. 'A little of what you fancy is good.'

Later we met some friends at Elaine's for a nightcap, then at 2 a.m. she announced she had to catch a 7 a.m. flight to Atlanta. 'But I'll be back the next day,' she said.

'You're a dynamo,' I said admiringly. 'You never stop.'

'Honey, if I'm not in the air I'm *on* the air,' Ivana quipped. 'And I'm never going to stop, believe me.'

I certainly do believe her. We made a date to meet on her boat in the summer and, with that, the invincible and inspirational Ivana was off into the warm May night.

Photographed by Eddie Sanderson at Ivana Trump's New York town house, 4 May 1998.

TWIGGY
THE FACE OF THE SWINGING SIXTIES

TWIGGY – THE VERY NAME instantly evokes 60s London at its trendiest and most exciting. The 'Me Generation' and the sudden explosion of youth culture was fuelled by the Beatles, mini-skirts, the final casting off of left-over restraints from the sedate 50s, and one skinny teenage girl.

If you were lucky enough to have been around in the 60s you might have spent some time in the King's Road, people-watching. The girls, or 'dollies' as they were called, looked divine – beehive hair-does augmented by pieces and wigs – artfully painted faces, eyelashes drawn *underneath* the eyes, and flowery mini dresses worn with sexy white go-go boots. Discotheques sprang up everywhere, as everyone danced the endless glorious nights away to the sounds of the Stones. The 60s were a dazzling decade, and no one epitomised that era more than a reed-thin 16-year-old called Twiggy.

Twiggy became the rage of London and the photographers' darling after her elfin features first graced the cover of *Vogue*. She had been living in Essex when a photographer spotted her and put her picture in the *Daily Express* and she soon became *the* face of 1965. On a June afternoon, thirty-three years later, we sat sipping tea in my London drawing room – she fresh from having her highlights done at Michaeljohn in Albemarle Street – me not-so-fresh, having jetted in that morning from LA.

Photographed by Steve Wood with Shakira Caine at London Fashion Week, 1994.

Nevertheless I soon perked up listening to 'Twigs', a down to earth, chirpy woman who still looks more like a girl. Her unmistakable face is little changed from when she first started modelling and she glows with health and high spirits. She also looks much younger than 48, and talks with infectious, easy-going charm. Happily married for thirteen years to actor Leigh Lawson, I asked Twiggy about personal life first.

'My daughter Carly is 19, from my first marriage, Leigh's got a 21-year-old son from when he was married to Hayley Mills and also a step-son, who was Hayley's boy by Roy Boulting.'

'You don't have a child together?'

'No, sadly, but I don't think I could cope with a baby now,' she giggled.

'Can you imagine being that woman of 61 who recently had a baby?' I asked.

'Oh my God! A great friend, Victoria Tennant, has just had her first baby at 47.'

'Forty-seven? In my mother's day that would have been unheard of, but happily nowadays more and more women are able to conceive later.'

'She had fertility treatments. She wanted this baby so much and she's coping well.'

'Don't you think that today, being in your forties and fifties and sixties is like being in your thirties and forties in Mama's time?' I asked.

'Absolutely. My Mum had me at 40. When she got pregnant, she was so cross she didn't talk to my Dad for three months. I was the last so everyone in the family spoilt me to death. Although now my Mum, God bless her, is 89 and has lost the plot a bit – she's probably on the verge of Alzheimer's.'

'Alzheimer's is such a terrifying disease, but it must be more terrifying for the family around the affected person. Was it she who called you Twiggy?'

'No, that was my first manager/boyfriend's brother. He used to call me Sticks, because of my legs, then suddenly one day Sticks turned into Twiggy. This was in the mid-60s when the *Daily Express* said "We name this girl the Face of '66" – that was it. I was off to New York and Paris and it was *mad*! I was a very young 16 from Neasden, like an Essex girl – kind of dumb, really.

'It was such a change of life overnight, and that's probably why it all just went over my head. It was like, "Yeah, this is it! This is marvellous" And I didn't stop. I hadn't had the ambition to be a model, so when it just happened it was great fun.'

'It went on for a long time.'

'Yeah. I modelled until 1970 when I met Ken Russell and he devised *The Boy Friend* for me. Once I'd done that film I didn't want to model anymore. I wasn't even a beauty, I was just odd looking, but I was kind of a *look*.'

'You had the biggest eyes I've ever seen, and weren't you the first person to wear false lower *eyelashes*?'

'Yes, I painted them on.'

'Which was the look of the late 60s – they became called twiggies. But do you think as one gets older one should wear less make-up?'

'I can't work or go out without my eyes on. I wear very little face make-up. I've got quite dry skin so I just use a very fine foundation from the Body Shop, I like the fact that they don't test on animals. I try to buy most of my make-up from places that don't experiment on animals. I put on a bit of rouge and do my eyes. I know the look now is very pale with no eye make-up but I couldn't do that, I need me eyes!'

'My daughter Katy doesn't wear any make-up at all except when I insist,' I said.

'Yeah, young girls don't anymore. It's a pity, really, 'cos it's fun. Carly only puts a tiny bit of mascara on – and they don't do anything with their hair – they just let it hang.'

'You've got good hair,' I said.

'It's really fine, but luckily I've got a lot of it. It's cut in layers and I just wash and blow-dry it dead straight, but with a bit of curl. I've got a hot air curling iron with spikes which is really good with this hairstyle.'

I asked her if she sunbathed.

'I love lying in the sun and reading but now we're all more aware of how bad it is I'm more careful. I don't actually like putting my face in the sun. I never have, and I think as you get older you shouldn't,' said Twiggy.

'I stopped when I was 21. I was working in Hollywood and I had a great tan, and with light eyes a tan looks really good – then a friend of mine said, "How can you do this to yourself? Come with me to the Beverly Hills Hotel and I'll show you shocking sights." So she took me by the pool for lunch and pointed to the lizard-like women with dark crocodile skins and said, "Do you want skin like that when you're 40?" I said '*no* way' and she said 'Then stop tanning your face now.' So I did.'

Twiggy shuddered. 'It's what happened to Bardot, isn't it? She's still extraordinary-looking, but she's dried up and aged terribly.'

If you had to go to a desert island and had only one cosmetic, what would it be?' I asked.

'My cold cream. I use a very cheap basic brand. It's only £5.95. I've tried all the posh expensive ones, which were useless because I've got really dry skin and this one is just glycerin and lanolin. When I went to live in America, where you can't buy it, I took a case with me.'

I asked Twiggy about her basic beauty routine.

'I always like to do some form of exercise. Leigh introduced me to the gym, but these past few months I fancied swimming, so I've been going to an Olympic-sized pool in a college sports club.'

'Don't they all recognise you and start yelling?'

'I just go in there with no make-up on and I've never been bothered. I put on a cap, and a nose pincher because I can't stand the water going in and I do thirty-two lengths, that's half a mile. It takes about thirty minutes. I try and do that twice a week – in the winter as well.'

'I wasn't ever a beauty, I was just odd looking, but I was kind of a look.'

The Boyfriend, *1971*.

'You are in great shape.'

'I was in better shape last summer. When I read all these diet and exercise books I feel like telling people if you want to lose weight and get fit do a play. When I did *Blithe Spirit* last summer, I was eating, drinking wine after the show and I *still* lost seven pounds. To lose weight – do a musical; it drops off you.'

'Do you work out with weights?'

'I'll do light weights, not heavy weights because I don't like that muscular look which a lot of LA actresses have, they almost look like men.'

'After you had a baby did you gain weight?'

'Until I was 29 I was really skinny and flat chested. Then after Carly I got my shape back pretty easily, but I felt that my body had changed and I started getting the figure that I'd always wanted but never had. When you're skinny, you always want to be more shapely. When Carly was 5 I went through a lot of stress with her father, and under stressful situations I eat. I was rehearsing as well as doing eight shows a week, tap-dancing, so I was really fit, and that's the best shape I've ever been in. I actually had quite a good figure, and it was all solid, none of these little spare tyres.' She grabbed a nonexistent spare tyre around her middle and giggled.

'Do you do stomach work?' I asked.

'Oh, that's the *worst*, it's what I find the hardest. After a baby, *everyone* has a tummy, don't they?'

'It gets like a balloon, but women mustn't stop eating and start doing thousands of sit-ups a day. You must build exercise up *slowly*,' I said.

'Absolutely,' said Twiggy. 'I can't stop eating, I like food too much. In the 60s I ate rubbish, and at 18 you can do that, particularly when you're built like I was. And of course we weren't into the health food kick. But a lot of people have problems with diet because they

go from one sort of eating to a crash diet like a yo-yo and it never works. You *must* teach yourself to eat properly. Maybe every two months I'll eat chips, but I *never* do fried food at home. We do stir-fried, but I only use olive oil to cook, never butter. The other good thing which I've discovered purely by experimenting is that you can actually stir-fry in soy sauce and white wine, and that's *completely* non-fattening. When you do a stir-fry, you can put anything in it – chicken and fish, but not red meat. I don't eat it because of the animal thing.'

'You're very into that, aren't you?' I asked.

'Yes, I feel very strongly about it. You are what you eat, that's important. You know, apart from losing the most wonderful friend in Linda McCartney we've also lost a woman who did an incredible amount for vegetarianism and animal ethics. She turned vegetarianism into a proper alternative.'

'Why does a woman who never drank or smoked and never ate meat contract breast cancer,' I asked.

'Linda ate and drank a *lot* of dairy. Now listen – I'm so upset about this – I've got a TV researcher looking into it because I think the truth about dairy products must be exposed. The awful thing about cow's milk is that farmers spray a pesticide called Lindane – which has been linked to breast cancer – on the food that the cattle eat. Twenty-three different pressure groups are urging the government to ban it. There was a documentary on the topic on British TV about four years ago, but for some reason nothing was done. They're still using this spray here on the feed and we've *got* to do something about it – we *must* always buy organic milk. I hope you do,' she said.

'No, I don't, but I will.'

'As soon as I heard about this documentary I just went ape. I rang *This Morning* and said I'd be happy to go on and say this is terrible, let's do something about it *now*. Did you know that

'My favourite de-stresser is a nice glass of red wine.'

England has one of the highest rates of breast cancer in Europe?'

'My mother *did* drink a lot of milk, and eat lots of cheese and butter, so maybe that did have something to do with it. Tests in America are now showing that diet is *incredibly* important and that being overweight after the menopause, makes you more liable to get breast cancer,' I said.

'Do you have check-ups?' Twiggy asked.

'Yes. If your mother had it, it's crucial. Let's change the subject. So, what do you do when you want to relax or de-stress, Twiggy?'

'I try to have a massage once a week. My masseuse is a brilliant osteopath as well, so she'll crack your bones. But my favourite de-stresser is a nice glass of red wine, round the telly having dinner with my lovely husband.'

'Pretty sexy, too,' I laughed.

'It is, yes.' She giggled like a teenager. 'We've been together for thirteen years. It took me long enough to find him. Nobody should ever give up looking, because I didn't think I'd ever meet anyone like Leigh, he's so wonderful. I was 35 when I met him, and he was 42. And of course he'd been split from Hayley for two years when we met, although he's still very friendly with her.'

'Hayley's father, John Mills, is amazing. He's over ninety. I was talking to him at a party recently and thought, whatever it is that he's doing, it *works*.'

'He's always followed the Hay Diet. I do admire people who are over ninety and fit. I want to live to be quite old.'

'So do I,' I said fervently. 'But only if the *quality* of my life is good – that's most important. I've interviewed a couple of women in their seventies who are *so* full of life and energy and still so active.'

'Keeping active is essential for mind *and* body,' Twiggy said.

'You're a terribly positive person. Do you have any negative things about you at all?' I asked.

'No,' she giggled. 'I don't really get depressed, thank God, probably because I had a wonderful childhood.'

'You have such a sunny disposition,' I said. 'Do you ever get cross?'

'Oh I get bad tempered. But not very often. If somebody's rude to me – the "You can't park here" syndrome – that makes me crazy.'

'Did you have heroines as a child?'

'I thought Fred Astaire was just the most beautiful thing I had ever seen. Nobody can move like Fred did. I loved his voice, and adored that kind of romantic 30s period. Of course, I was very much a 60s girl – that's why I'm doing the Noel Coward. It was through Ken Russell, who was a great film buff, that I got hooked. He was an education – my mentor really, because I left school at 16 and I knew nothing about the film business.'

'So what's your main secret you'd like to pass onto other women?' I asked.

'Try to laugh and be happy most of the time, that keeps you young and healthy. Have a wonderful partner, be kind and be good. I try – I don't always pull it off.' She laughed heartily.

'I bet you do – you certainly *look* like you do,' I said. We walked to my front door and hugged and I watched her lightly trip down the stairs. Twiggy turned and gave a cheery wave and I thought what a truly happy, truly pretty woman. Looking as good as when she was the darling of the 60s, she is obviously totally fulfilled in whatever she does.

FOUR HOSTESSES WITH THE MOSTEST

BETSY BLOOMINGDALE, AUDREY WILDER, LYNN WYATT AND SANDRA DI PORTANOVA

There is a certain type of woman, indigenous to the Western world, who is well-known, popular and widely respected and yet doesn't have a career, in the strictest sense of the word. Women such as this just *are*. I am in no way negating these ladies' contributions to life for in many ways they contribute heavily, though charities and by being tremendous life enhancers.

Women who 'do nothing' are often derided for their hedonism or narcissism but in the case of these four women, I consider them not only great friends but also great hostesses and women I admire enormously.

Betsy Bloomingdale

IF THE BILLY WILDERS are Hollywood Royalty, then Betsy Bloomingdale is the Queen of social Los Angeles. Mother of three and grandmother of eight, the former Betsy Newling has survived, with enormous dignity, misfortunes and scandals that would have crushed lesser mortals. Swanning gloriously through the salons of Beverly Hills, New York and Paris, Betsy Bloomingdale's poise and glamour puts women half her age to shame. Always exquisitely groomed, Betsy has been on the best-dressed list many times, and is now in their hall of fame. She is also one of the best hostesses in America.

Betsy serves on several committees involving art, is on the visiting committee of the Costume Council of the Metropolitan Museum of Art in New York, and Friends of Art and Preservation in Embassies in Washington DC. She has served on the President's Committee on the Arts and the Humanities and is a founding member of The James Madison National Council of The Library of Congress.

Betsy's closest friend is Nancy Reagan and I have often seen them lunching or dining together. Betsy and her late husband Alfred were part of the Reagan Kitchen Cabinet when Betsy was known as 'The First Friend'. A close-knit group of Los Angeles-based Republican tycoons, including Walter and Lee Annenberg and Marion and Earle Jorgenson, they were an

Photographed by Eddie Sanderson at Betsy's home in Holmby Hills, California, 12 May 1998.

extremely powerful group who propelled Ronald Reagan into the White House and still remain his closest inner core. Today, as Reagan fights Alzheimer's disease, Betsy is still Nancy's closest confidante and a tower of strength to her, as was obvious when I lunched with them both recently.

Betsy wrote a stunning book, *Entertaining with Betsy Bloomingdale*, in which she shared her secrets for creating great menus and entertaining. One of her axioms is 'You can have all the money and privilege in the world yet have no style – and you can spend fortunes on the most lavish parties and leave your guests feeling bored and let down. Every woman can be a great hostess if she possesses and expresses warmth, attention to detail, creativity, genuine caring and joy in life. *Real* style comes from within.'

Betsy Bloomingdale certainly has masses of style. On a freezing cold, rainy May day Betsy was wearing an elegant pearl grey pinstripe Valentino suit and a white lace blouse complemented by a row of large, perfect grey pearls. Her make-up and ash-blonde hair were immaculate, her look that of a true European/American sophisticate.

Her sumptuous Palladian-style Holmby Hills home built in the late 1950s has, like Mrs Bloomingdale herself, a quiet elegance and refinement. It has been the setting for many wonderful dinners, lunches and drinks parties and I always marvelled at Betsy's skill as the consummate hostess, putting guests at their ease and serving non-showy but exquisite food. It was only logical that my first question would be to ask her what she considered the secret of great entertaining.

'As a hostess you must have everything arranged beforehand so when the doorbell rings you can go to your own party. If something goes wrong – dinner is late or someone spills red wine on your pale carpet – turn the other cheek and pay *no* attention. After every detail has been carefully supervised – relax and enjoy it.'

'Some people think parties are a waste of time,' I said.

'Entertaining is one of the great essentials of life.'

'I believe entertaining is one of the great essentials of life. One of our most *basic* human needs is to bring pleasure to others by sharing one's home and table and giving of oneself – beautifully prepared food can be an inspiration. Parties are not frivolous. Think of all the things that happen at them. How many marriages are born there? How many lifelong friends made? The essence of entertaining well is to share our houses and open our hearts to people we care for and admire.'

'What if something ghastly happens – for example, if the lights fuse so the dinner won't cook?' I asked.

Betsy laughed. 'This actually happened to us once. I just sent Alfred out for a big tub of Kentucky Fried Chicken and we all had a great time. Giving a dinner or party is, in many ways, like a performance. *You* are the producer, director and finally the actor. Think of a party as a drama and set the stage perfectly to create the mood. Flowers, lighting and table settings are the props, which create an ambience – doing something just a *tiny* bit different will make your party successful.'

I asked how she kept her wonderful complexion and she answered, 'I was taught by Erno Laszlo years ago. I put Laszlo's oil on my face, then wash with his soap and pat on his night cream. Finally, I splash about thirty times which is the classic Erno Laszlo technique. Do you know, if you went to him and were ten minutes late he wouldn't bother to see you, *whoever* you might be! Many people have tried to copy his products and Janet Sartin's is probably the closest... I use her things too... she used to be a nurse for Dr Laszlo, then moved onto her own line. I even took my daughter to Dr Laszlo when she was 14.'

'You don't seem to wear much foundation,' I said.

'I use Janet Sartin's base, because it's wonderfully light, and then Mac on top of it,' she said. 'Then I use lipstick and shadow. Vassilis, a nice Greek boy, taught me all *sorts* of make-up tricks, because when I did QVC I wanted to do my own make-up better than the make-up people assigned to me did. It only takes me about ten minutes. I love make-up. I don't like to look at myself in the morning without it,' she laughed.

The butler brought us tea in an exquisite Limoges service, along with a divine cake made from Betsy's own recipe, and we moved on to discuss exercise and diet.

'I am very, *very* serious about exercise but I do *not* believe in going to the gym and sweating and straining for an hour and a half. I don't think that that's good for women,' Betsy said vehemently.

'I *don't* believe in stringent dieting,' she continued, 'but I do actually weigh myself every day because I can't *stand* it if I go up a pound then down a pound. For a while I was

two or three pounds overweight and my exercise man, Mike Abrams, gave me a twenty-minute routine to do while watching the news. I'm not someone who can get to a gym every day. I'll *never* do it, and I'll *never* go running. I don't even go to the park to walk. If I can't do it at home I don't want to do it. I've got some great, easy to do stomach exercises.'

'Keeping a flat tummy is practically impossible, particularly if you've had children,' I ruefully remarked.

'Practically impossible, yes, but here's an excellent exercise,' said Betsy. 'Sit in a chair, lift your feet up off the ground and *hold* it. That'll kill you and keep it in check! And when you're driving and come to a stop signal think "tuck in". Then you get another stop sign and it's tuck in again – it works. And I also had these marvellous arm exercises. Two years ago I bought a cute little Chanel sleeveless dress. Friends said, "You're *so* lucky you can still wear a sleeveless dress". Then when I broke my wrist, I couldn't do the push-ups and the skin on my arms started sagging. Robert at Chanel in New York said, "Why don't you just have your arms tucked?" I was horrified and said I would *never* do that. But I asked him if people really have their arms tucked, and he said yes.'

She looked slightly shocked so I told her one of my friends has actually had it done. 'But I do think that this is one of the problems of the over-50s,' I continued. 'Shirley Bassey has the most incredible arms but she does two hours in the gym with weights *every single day*. There has to be an answer to this because it's one of those problem areas that all women have.'

'Now my dresses always have a little sleeve or something just in here...' Betsy motioned to her shoulders.

'You've got a fantastically smooth cleavage, Betsy – you've obviously never been in the sun.' She nodded vigorously.

'My mother told me to *never* put my face in

the sun. But I get brown hands and legs in the summer, since I put everything in except my face. I always wear a big hat and *now* I know why some elderly ladies like Brooke Astor wear gloves to hide their hands,' she chuckled.

'But you don't seem to have any sun damage, at all,' I said.

'I freckle. I play tennis every Sunday in like a dirndl up to *here*, with long sleeves. It can be a hundred degrees but I still wear long sleeves.'

'But you have an *extraordinary* décolletage.'

'That's with the help of the marvellous skin doctor Doctor Orentreich in New York. I was told about him by Merle Oberon. He's better than anyone out here. He gave me some cream to put on my chest and now the skin's quite clear,' she said.

'It's not just clear, Betsy, it's *fantastic.*'

She smiled and promised to send me some of Doctor Orentreich's cream. I then asked her how she de-stressed.

'I'm happy just having dinner at home by myself. I have a very nice beau, which is fine, but part of me wants to be alone. I play tennis every Sunday, then soak in my bathtub, have brunch and get into a big old terrycloth robe. With luck I'm not going out to dinner, but if I am it's later that evening. Then I just sort of flake and watch television, potter in my garden which I adore and read the Sunday papers. I

never put make-up on.'

I asked her if she could only take one beauty product with her on a desert island what would it be?

'I think I'd like to take a little make-up kit because I'd be the only person around to look at, so I better look good,' she joked.

'Who are your heroes or heroines? People you admire?' I asked.

'I *adored* Merle Oberon. She was a great beauty and she had such an alluring way with people. She'd get Alfred Bloomingdale to do *anything* she wanted. Merle would say "Alfred stop that. You can't smoke in here" and he'd stop. She'd make us take our shoes off to walk on the carpet because she was so immaculate. Everything she did in her houses here and in Acapulco was exquisite. She had marvellous skin; in spite of *always* being in the sun, but she *was* Anglo-Indian. She often wore white strapless dresses with a beautiful turquoise necklace.'

'You've been voted one of the best-dressed women in the world but we now live in a time when for a woman to be called glamorous or pretty is almost like a dirty word. What do *you* think is the secret of looking good – since one can't wear turquoises and white strapless dresses anymore?' I said.

'No, you can't wear that anymore but I believe that you *can* look fabulous and I do

'I said, "I'd better put on some jeans", and Ronaldo Hererra said, "Why?" I said "This suit is a little dressy for Soho, isn't it?" he answered "Betsy, don't disappoint people, they expect you to dress up."'

believe that you *can* knock people out. Renaldo Hererra said something to me that has stuck in my mind. I was in New York lunching with him and Carolina and I was going to take my grandson to Balthazar for dinner in Soho and I said, "I'd better put on some jeans", and Renaldo Hererra said "Why?". I said, "This suit is a little dressy for Soho, isn't it?" and he answered "Betsy, *don't* disappoint people, they *expect* you to dress up." She laughed.

'That's good advice,' I said. 'I mean, you don't have to wear some silver strapless thing, but you *can* still dress up. You do and I do. I loved the way my mother and my aunts used to dress – all the hats, the veils, gloves and fitted suits of the 40s and 50s. To accentuate your body almost seems a crime these days unless you're under 30. Also I don't think most women have the figures for it anymore.'

'Because so many women are terribly overweight,' agreed Betsy.

'So they just stick to baby-gros,' I laughed. 'But today's designers don't help any of us. Look at how we're dressed. We're in simple pant suits, and practically *every* woman I've interviewed has been wearing a simple tailored suit. The fashion pundits and magazines, on the other hand, are all saying *don't* wear tailored things, wear a slip dress or a cardigan and a long floaty skirt.'

'Never,' shuddered Betsy. We both agreed we loved Valentino's clothes and while Betsy poured more tea I asked her the secret of her fabulous hair.

'George Masters cut my hair this way, very short at the back and then long at the front, years ago. I've kept that look for ages. It might be a little bit longer, a little bit shorter but you know it is something that belongs to you. It's thick and I've always believed that if you find something that is the right style for you, you shouldn't change it. The Duchess of Windsor, who was a chic although not really terribly attractive woman, always had that same marvellous hairstyle that was flattering to her face,' she said.

'The Jennifer Anniston generation change their hairstyle every week,' I said. 'I know you knew Claudette Colbert. I saw her in Barbados a year before she died and she still had the same hairstyle. It was amazing because her hair was grey but still extremely thick.' Then I asked Betsy for her philosophy to looking fabulous and having such joie de vivre. 'Mrs Astor once said "I get rid of my friends every year; the ones that are boring I just decide not to see them anymore." Do you think like that?' I asked her.

'It happens,' she replied. 'I have been lucky in having fabulous children, as are their husbands and wives. I went out with them the other night, Mother's Day, to Spago with the children – *that* keeps you in a different group. That's very important, because you can get stuck just seeing your own little circle, especially in this town. If you're unhappy or miserable about something, stay *home*, don't go out and inflict your moods on your friends. They might say "Oh, too bad you're sad," but they couldn't care *less*. So unless it's a close friend who understands – don't go. People really *don't* want to spend time saying, "Oh you poor thing, I'm sorry."'

It was time for Eddie to take our picture. We couldn't go into the gorgeous garden as the rain was bucketing down so we posed on Betsy's beautiful terrace, with the rain as our backdrop, spattering our pale grey suits. Betsy took it all with great good humour and as we left, with promises to meet in the South of France, Eddie said, 'People could learn so much from that lady because she *truly* is a lady. The essence of charm, sophistication and warmth.'

'And a fabulous hostess, too,' I said.

Audrey Wilder

I FIRST SAW THE DAZZLING Audrey Wilder on my initial Hollywood go-round at the house of super-agent Charles Feldman. She was sitting on a sofa in front of the Matisse – *soignée* in a black strapless dress, smoking a cigarette and flanked by Richard Burton and Cary Grant, who were clearly entranced by her.

I thought Audrey Wilder the epitome of sophisticated chic (still do), and watched her admiringly from across a room filled with the likes of Merle Oberon, Judy Garland and George Cukor. Heady stuff, but I sat back and just observed.

A few months later we met again at Gene Kelly's house. Audrey was with her brilliant writer-director husband Billy, and was charming, witty and wise, not to mention shockingly beautiful and devastatingly elegant. She was in fact far better groomed and put together than most of the celebrated actresses there.

Over the past ten years Audrey and I have become close friends and I wouldn't dream of visiting California without calling the Wilders and dining together either at a restaurant or at their exquisite apartment.

On a hot May night we dined on the terrace of the Bel Air Hotel with Billy and Robin. Audrey was looking divine in an ink-blue Ralph Lauren pant suit and white shirt, her trademark Chanel gardenia in her lapel, her black 'Louise Brooks' bob impeccable. As we talked she chain smoked, a habit which is rather difficult to maintain in rigidly anti-smoking California. She ate heartily: artichoke salad, lamb with all the trimmings and a fine dessert. She drank vodka with water and obviously has no weight problems.

Since Audrey is always exquisitely dressed I wanted to know her style secrets, so I asked her what would be her perfect wardrobe for a week-long trip.

'I'd take three or four pairs of black pants in different textures and two or three jackets in different weights, and then a pair of white crêpe pants. For going out at night, it's easy – you just put on pearls and jewellery, with the jacket. One jacket should be made of satin or silk, also black or white so you don't need to carry coloured accessories. Besides, coloured bags and shoes are the *worst*. I always wear jackets, slacks and shirts but the shirts *must* be drip dry. Spending money on dry cleaning is a waste and I detest ironing. If you search the big medium-priced department stores like Robertson-May in LA, Macys in New York or Selfridges in London you'll always be able to root out a great drip dry blouse.'

'What do you think is the key to style?' I asked.

'The most important thing is to know what type you are. It's very important to know *what* you look like, because I know so many people who don't have a *clue*.'

'I went to this Country and Western party a few years ago with a friend; when I turned up she was wearing this Pucci outfit – patterned tights and a long jacket with fringes. I said to her "Take that back. You look ridiculous... it's a Western party, tie a scarf round your neck and put on a white shirt." Then I went back to the shop and said "Who sold that outfit to Mrs X?" but, of course, everyone denied it.'

'Shop assistants will sell you anything,' added. 'They're there to sell, not to be honest.'

'You've got to keep it simple,' reiterated Audrey, 'and don't be seduced by things that

aren't right for you, just because they're trendy.'

'Do you have any heroines?' I asked.

'My mother was a heroine to me, and I don't mean that facetiously. She was a terrific woman who worked very hard and protected me and she made many of my clothes right up until she died.'

'What would you say was your philosophy of life?' I asked.

'Keep on truckin'.' She laughed her smoky laugh and lit another Virginia Slim. 'What's the use of loading off on anybody? I avoid people who are a pain in the ass if I can. *Everybody* in life has problems, some big, some small. I can't say I've had any huge problems or anything like that, but I *have* been a care-giver to a lot of people. You've got to do it when you've got to do it, that's all. People think I don't do anything, but I do all my own marketing and cooking and Billy's a full-time job,' she laughed.

'So how do you de-stress?' I asked her.

'I take a nap,' she smiled, 'that can solve a *lot* of problems! And as for food, I eat *everything*, hamburgers, hot dogs, desserts – in fact I'm trying to put on weight. I'm not one of those tits and ass blonde types.'

I asked her about exercise.

'I walk, walk, walk. I walk around the market every day searching for the freshest produce, and cooking's quite energetic.'

'Do you feel happier now than you did in your twenties and thirties?'

'It's a different kind of happiness. When I was 20 I was singing with Tommy Dorsey's band. Those were great days. Then in my thirties I married Billy and have lived this great life, which has more or less continued.'

'You look so wonderful and cope with getting older fantastically well. Did you start thinking about it when you were very young?'

'No. I've always tried to have the best time I can. I try not to worry about the future because there's not a damn thing you can do about anything. I smoke and I drink vodka and of course I have responsibilities – Billy and my brother. But I believe if you're lucky enough to have the wherewithal to have "a good life" you'd better enjoy that life 'cos too many people out there are suffering a lot.'

Sound advice from a woman in her seventies who truly looks amazing. Happily married for over forty years, the Wilders are still Hollywood royalty and she continues to entertain beautifully at their apartment.

As the song says, 'She's a very stylish girl'.

'What would you say was your philosophy of life?' I asked. 'Keep on truckin,' said Audrey.

Photographed with her husband Billy Wilder by Richard Young, London, 1992.

Lynn Wyatt

AFTER YET ANOTHER OF her brilliant parties I talked to Lynn Wyatt in her charming house with a spectacular view of St Jean Cap Ferrat. Lynn is one of the most prolific and accomplished of hostesses and for the past twenty-five years she has thrown a 16 July birthday bash for herself to which the movers and shakers of Monaco, Cap Ferrat and St. Tropez flock. The party's theme changes every year. This year it was Asian chic; a few years ago it was denim 'n' diamonds and she's had a white theme, a gold theme and a gipsy theme.

Lynn's tables are always beautifully laid; each one with a separate theme. For her last party each table was given the name of a Riviera town. When she gave a dinner for me in Houston several years ago, each table had the name of one of my books – *Prime Time, Second Act* etc. Lynn leaves no stone unturned in her quest for perfection and her guest list reflects that. Guests often include Elton John, Jack Nicholson, Roger Moore, Michael Caine, Helmut Newton, Shirley Bassey, Jerry Hall, Prince Rainier and Prince Albert of Monaco, Karl Lagerfeld, Liza Minnelli, and many more.

It was a hot August morning, and Lynn was stunning in tight white pants and a black peasant blouse, when I asked her 'What is your secret for giving a great party?'

'My secret is to think of all the details of the party first. Think of everything that *can* happen, that *will* happen and then plan extensively – everything from beginning to end.'

'Do you think guests are important?' I asked.

'The mixture of guests is one of the most important things to get right in advance, then the minute the first guest walks in the door I forget about it and enjoy myself at my own parties.'

'Do you mix people up by ages? Would you, say, put a seventy-year-old next to a twenty-year-old?'

'It depends solely on the person. I try to think what different people have to offer each other. Is this person going to be amused by this other person? If it's a man who likes pretty girls but the girl doesn't have that much to say then I won't necessarily seat them together... that's why I *agonise* over my placement. I don't mind putting one girl next to another if they're interesting. Often there's many more women than men.

I asked Lynn about her beauty secrets.

'My beauty-skin regime begins with a topical Vitamin C Skin Firming cream mixed with two drops of Hydrating B5 Moisture Gel (which I get from my dermatologist in Houston). That's followed by a moisturising Sun-Bloc, concealer, then Dior foundation. After the bath I apply Cocoa Butter moisturising cream all over my body which I buy at the drugstore. It's the best thing for softening tough, dry skin.

I vary my day and night creams for the face and neck every three months as well as daily cleansers but I use Pure Rose Water as a toner without fail and I've always believed make-up is a *great* protector.'

'How about exercise?' I asked.

'In Texas during one week I have three different trainers who each have their own routine for me. I believe one's muscles get used to the

Photographed by Nicola Formby at Lynn's house in Cap Ferrat, 3 August 1998.

same exercises so one must have variety – plus it keeps it interesting. I do strength-training, strenuous aerobics, stretching (before and after exercising), toning, Kundalini Yoga and I'm a first degree Black Belt in the martial art Tae Kwon Do.

'When travelling I try to do extensive stretching and a bit of jumping rope (a real fat burner) on my own.'

I asked if Lynn had any special diet or eating secrets.

'What secrets!!??' she laughed. 'I really love good food and am not one of those girls that push food around on their plate. I have a true weakness for sweets so when desserts are in front of me I eat all of them *plus* my neighbour's. When I'm at home my chef prepares wonderful low-calorie tasty meals and *no* desserts. Then if I 'pig-out' two or three days in a row, I skip lunch and drink lots of water, water, water and freshly made vegetable juice. I believe in drinking water at room temperature. It goes down faster (drink it, don't sip it) and it doesn't shock the system.'

'You've been voted to the International Best Dressed Hall of Fame,' I said. 'What are your beliefs in dressing well?'

'The most important words to me in dressing well are, "What is appropriate?" What is appropriate for the occasion as well as for my age? I always consider these options even if an outfit looks well okay me and I love it. I love accessories and think the way one puts together certain accessories makes the style of the individual. One beauty product a woman should *never* forsake is a mirror. The mirror doesn't lie so respect its wisdom.'

'I guess my vanity is showing because I would never consider leaving my house without "my face on",' Lynn continued. 'Even at our ranch I'll apply sunscreen, concealer and foundation to protect my skin and a little lip gloss so as not to frighten the animals!'

'What are your views on ageing?' I asked.

'I seldom think of anyone's age,' she said emphatically. 'I don't count my own birthdays but I sure do celebrate them! I feel every age has its own growth process and learning experiences so I try to progress mentally and spiritually as well as physically.'

'What beauty product would you take if wrecked on a desert island?' I asked her.

'I never sit in the sun so I'd take sun-bloc... and then some more sun-bloc.' She laughed.

'And how do you de-stress and relax?'

'In the short term: take three deep breaths focusing on exhaling all your negative thoughts. But in the long term I think meditation, yoga and a good book are the best ways to keep stress levels down.'

Sound advice from a woman who enjoys a richly fulfilled life and whose philosophy is: 'Live life as an adventure, continue to learn and be profoundly grateful for the gifts you have been given.'

Lynn Wyatt – a beautiful and charming woman who has many gifts and gives joy to numerous people, not to mention spectacular parties.

Sandra di Portanova

ANDRA DI PORTANOVA IS NOT only beautiful but one of the wittiest women I know. She's famous for her bons mots as well as her exceptional skills as an internationally renowned hostess.

I've stayed with Sandra and her husband Enrico, both in Acapulco and Houston, many times and have never failed to be impressed by her tireless efforts in throwing spectacular dinner parties. These can range from dinner for ten with delicious home-made pasta, often cooked by Ricky, to star-studded charity bashes for seven hundred held on the roof of their extraordinary villa in Acapulco which has enough space for three helicopters to land.

Sandra Hovis was born in Houston, Texas in the late forties. She met Baron Enrico di Portanova just after graduating from college and they were married a few months later. Twenty-five years later they are still, as Sandra says, 'madly in love.' At their glamorous 25th wedding anniversary in Monte Carlo in July their devotion to each other was much in evidence.

A week later I met Sandra for lunch at the Colombe d'Or restaurant in St. Paul de Vence. She was, as usual, a vision in a canary yellow pant suit and white straw hat. In spite of the amount of time she spends in sunny climes Sandra never sun-bathes and has the creamy skin and jet black hair of a true Southern Belle and a curvaceous womanly figure with a 'belle poitrine'.

We ordered the delicious hors d'oeuvres and Petal de Rose wine and I asked her:

'Do you believe in make-up as a protector?'

'*Absolutely...* to protect against other women!' she quipped.

'What is your exercise regime?'

'Sporadic. I'll start doing all sorts of things but usually I'll put something out of joint! But I *do* like sports. Especially Paddle tennis.'

'I've never seen you swim.'

'I'll have water aerobics with an instructor usually for the guests. We all get in there and splash around, it's very good for you and it's much better, water aerobics, than regular aerobics.'

'Regular aerobics are *terrible* for you, they are proving that more and more today,' I said.

'I know you like your food, Sandra, and you have a good body. You're not thin but you wouldn't look good stick thin.'

'That's what I keep telling my husband,' she laughed. 'I'm afraid it's fast or feast. If I go on a feast, then I have to fast.'

'What are your beliefs about dressing well?'

'I think the old adage: you really can't go wrong with the famous little black dress for all occasions. When in doubt pull that out.'

'I've seen your closet. You have an enormous amount of clothes. How do you weed out, or don't *you*?'

'I raise money for the the Amigos d'Acapulco charity, by having auctions of my clothes. I thought this is a wonderful way I can recycle things to people who'd enjoy them, and also raise some money for the orphans. Everybody seems to enjoy it so I end up giving a big party twice a year and invite friends over and they can get things, if not for themselves, then for their friends. The charity helps the six orphanages and the day-care centre hospital for out-patients and it gives scholarships to children. We have the Joan Collins Scholarship that we've created in your honour

by the way, for little girls with talent who achieve higher scholastic ability. Sylvester Stallone came and helped us and Henry Kissinger and many other celebrities,' she said.

'Your home in Acapulco is without doubt one of the most beautiful and fantastic houses in the world and you always have such exciting parties and glamorous guests... How many parties do you have each season?'

'I'll probably have one or two charities. This year I'm doing one at Christmas for the New Acapulco Philharmonic Orchestra. I can have the whole orchestra there plus about five hundred guests,' she said.

'I know you plan and organise it *all* yourself and you've always had this incredible knack of setting the most inventive and fantastic tables.'

'I call them my tablescapes,' she smiled.

'Can you describe what you do?'

'If you have something rather interesting, whether it's fantastical or just very elegant or simple it is a great conversational ice-breaker. It's like showtime. So let's see; I had the gold theme for Placido Domingo. Each table was set as a particular opera that he had sung... there were seven tables of ten and I had a photograph of every single person, in a costume from that opera, in a silver frame,' she said.

'Amazing,' I said. 'And incredibly time consuming. How did you do it?'

'I went through several opera books, made photocopies, cut out the heads of the people from a photograph and stuck them on. It's amusing because each person has a little cadeau they can remember. I also had fans for each table. For the Madame Butterfly table it was easy, I had oriental fans and the others were all different but thematic. If I'm doing a party like that I'm very detailed.'

Photographed by Nicola Formby at the Colomb d'Or restaurant, Saint Paul de Vence, France, 4 August 1998.

'Do you have any key entertaining do's and dont's?' I asked.

'I would never seat three women or three men together at dinner. There's no excuse for that. It's just lazy hosting and rather insulting to the person in the middle. If you *have* invited several extra men or women it's acceptable to sit two together. It's also completely incorrect to sit husbands and wives, or partners, together. They see enough of each other at home – give them someone else to talk to.'

'At your anniversary last week you gave everybody a camera, and on one side of the camera box was a photo of you and Ricky *now* and the other side, twenty-five years ago.'

'I thought the cameras would be fun because everyone wants photographs from a party that's rather glamorous, and then I don't have to worry about getting photographs for two hundred people.'

I told Sandra that during her party many of the guests said she looked only twenty-five now.

'Bless you,' she smiled. 'Those friends need glasses!'

'But you *do* look so young. What's your secret?'

'I don't try to stay too thin,' she said. 'I believe a little roundness is much more youthful.'

I remarked that often women over forty who have dieted rigidly had many more wrinkles than those who enjoyed their food and I asked her how she kept such wonderful skin.

'Every day Sun-bloc 50 with moisturiser, under make-up. La Prairie eye creams – Chanel foundation. Facial masque two or three times a week and then every night I use Fabiella eye-make-up remover and apply eye cream and moisturiser.'

'So on a desert island you'd choose...'

'Sun-Bloc, Sun-Bloc, Sun-Bloc!' she chuckled.

I asked Sandra who her heroes or heroines were and she replied without hesitation:

'Adversity must be taken on and not ignored – fight it.'

'I'm romantic so my Number One hero is my husband. It was love at first sight. He was the most handsome man I've ever met and has a great heart. He's also very honourable and creative and I'm his heroine too.'

'As for heroines – Clare Booth Luce. She wrote *The Women* and married one of the world's most powerful men but she did her own thing very successfully and I adore and admire Beverly Sills, the opera singer. She's enormously talented, fantastic fun to be with, *extremely* intelligent and wise. Finally Barbara Walters who broke the mould in her field and is still doing it. I'm a great admirer of people who keep on breaking moulds and who manage to survive. I *love* survivors.'

I asked Sandra her philosophy of life and she answered, 'The good old golden rule is to do unto others as you'd have them do to you and love thy neighbour. You can't do better than to live by that.'

I told her that she has clearly succeeded in living by that rule, as she was enormously kind, very generous and deeply loved.

'I'm also optimistic,' she said. 'Even if something bad happens, I try and turn it into something positive. I'm not really Pollyanna but I try to look for the silver lining and if you look for it you often find it. We *all* have adversity in our lives but you can't dwell on it. Everyone has different ways of coping but I use prayer. When my husband had cancer we didn't tell anyone at first but we had to confront it. I said, "This is a war and we are going to win it." I am more of a fighter than he is. Adversity must be taken on and not ignored – fight it. If you *do* find something life-threatening happening to you – do not give up. Find the best doctors and beat it.'

'A positive attitude is also the greatest beauty secret,' she continued. 'Your attitude can change your face. When you frown you *lose* beauty – when you smile and *think* you're pretty – you are. People who think bad thoughts – it shows on their faces.'

I agreed, then Sandra said, 'I also have a very convenient memory. I don't hold grudges. One can't go through life with one's friends and loved ones without having the occasional squall or misunderstanding. You pass this way *once* so you might as well do what you want. That's why Ricky and I live an international life. Because we *truly* enjoy it.'

'And long may you do so,' I said. We posed for our pictures on the terrace of the Colombe d'Or to the amusement of the rest of our lunch guests, then said goodbye with promises to meet in Acapulco in the New Year.

Sandra di Portanova is truly a life enhancer. An immensely charismatic, amusing and strong woman who is also deeply feminine and romantic; a fabulous hostess and a very good friend.

MY FRIENDS' ESSENTIAL SECRETS

IN THIS PENULTIMATE CHAPTER I've distilled my friends' advice and philosophies down to key points in four areas, so that you can see at a glance their varying beauty secrets.

Remember, not everyone's advice will be identical. The real secret is to remember that we are all different and to pick the path to vitality and beauty that suits you best.

Whilst some of my friends' sentiments are quite different, there are ten essential key points on which we nearly all agree:

1 Health is more important than anything else; with optimum health vitality and youthfulness will follow.

2 Think positive.

3 No sunbathing or smoking.

4 The importance of eating healthy and pure food.

5 Looking good means finding a style that suits you, and not trying to emulate anyone else.

6 The need to be aware of impurities in food, the air we breathe and everyday products.

7 Frequent but sensible exercise. Overdoing exercise can be as harmful as not doing any at all.

8 The need to maintain a sensible weight through moderate eating and exercise rather than crash diets.

9 The value of thorough and careful skin care; deep cleansing, moisturising and sun-bloc.

10 The power of make-up to protect and enhance.

BEAUTY

■ A quick blast of cold water, after a hot shower, does wonders for the skin and circulation.

Shirley Bassey

■ Specially blended foundation, which matches your skin tone, is worth the extra time and money.

Shirley Bassey

■ Enjoy the act of putting on make-up. It's an art form, a chance to be creative with your face.

Shirley Bassey

■ To aid dry skin add a quarter of a litre of milk and a few drops of pure vegetable oil, such as sesame or apricot oil, to your bath water.

Diahann Carroll

■ Be realistic about your looks. If you want plastic surgery, go for it, but be careful not to overdo it.

Diahann Carroll

■ The mirror is the best beauty aid. It never lies, so do buy a good, full length, three-way mirror... and use it!

Diahann Carroll

■ If you don't like the feel of foundation on your skin, but want a little protection and coverage, you can always use moisturiser, concealer and a touch of powder instead.

Arlene Dahl

■ Homemade egg facemasks are excellent for dry skin. Beat two eggs, then apply them to the face with cotton wool. Relax, allow them to harden, then rinse off with warm water. If your skin's really dry, use only the egg yolks.

Arlene Dahl

■ Accept your age and your figure and accentuate the positives. Create a flattering silhouette by disguising the problem areas and drawing attention to your favourable ones.

Arlene Dahl

■ The best beauty treatment is smiling!
Angie Dickinson

■ After a certain age it doesn't suit most women to be too thin.
Angie Dickinson

■ Sunscreen is the most essential of all health and beauty items.

Morgan Fairchild

■ New scientific skin-care developments and products are materialising all the time, so keep up to date with them.

Morgan Fairchild

■ Look to women of the past – the Edwardian era and the 1950s in particular – for inspiration on looking truly pretty.

Joanna Lumley

■ Don't be intimidated by fashion. Sit out any trends that don't flatter you.

Ali McGraw

■ If you want to look tanned, *fake it*! There are several excellent long-lasting fake tanning products on the market.

Stefanie Powers

■ Beauty products don't have to be expensive to be effective. Carefully selected, the local chemist's products can be as good as the most exclusive department store's.

Stefanie Powers

■ Find a daily and nightly beauty routine that works for you and never, ever neglect it.

Michelle Philips

■ Navy blue eyeliner on the inside of the bottom eye-lid makes eyes look whiter and brighter.

Morgan Fairchild

■ Most women over 40 look better with shorter hair.

Morgan Fairchild

■ If you're over 40 but don't want to cut your hair, then put it up and if you want a different look one evening then experiment with a hair piece or even a wig.

Louise Fennell

■ Don't *ever* blow dry your hair, use nylon combs or brushes or over-wash it; the natural oils are good for it.

Jerry Hall

■ Cleanse your face carefully, regularly. Always use clean towels.

Joan Rivers

■ Eyeliner is the most effective item of make-up for the majority of women.

Joan Rivers

■ Be realistic about plastic surgery. It works but you need to find a good surgeon and remember that the results need to be maintained. The bonus will be a big boost in self-esteem.

Joan Rivers

You don't have to be young or pretty to look glamorous. It's all about developing your own style.

Joan Rivers

Try and enjoy every minute of your life and look the best you can *all* the time.

Joan Rivers

Don't overdo the make-up; too much can be ageing.

Alana Stewart

Women with sensitive skin should avoid acidic exfoliators.

Alana Stewart

The 1990s fashion for no eye make-up doesn't suit all of us. Those of us who like eye make-up should keep on using it.

Twiggy

Make-up is a great protector... especially against other women.

Baroness Sandra di Portanova

Pure rose water is a wonderful toner and coconut butter is the best all-over-body moisturising cream.

Lynn Wyatt

Know your type, never try to be something you're not and realise that sales assistants are there to sell, not to tell the truth about how you look.

Audrey Wilder

HEALTH

Be aware of the toxins that enter your bloodstream just through everyday living and eating.

Jacqueline Bisset

Be aware of your body – make sure you have regular health checks. Thanks to this I found out very early on that I had breast cancer.

Diahann Carroll

Hormone Replacement Therapy isn't just beneficial to the bones, but to your skin and your vitality too.

Diahann Carroll

Avoid faddy or crash diets – your body is a chemistry lab and certain components are essential for its correct functioning.

Morgan Fairchild

Try the anti-diet; eat all you can, but *never* eat between meals and avoid flour and white sugar.

Louise Fennell

■ Proper food is the best source of nutrition; avoid taking too many vitamin supplements unless under doctor's orders.

Louise Fennell

■ Be aware of how certain foods make you feel; then you can pinpoint those that cause an adverse reaction, like weight gain and bloating.

Fiona Fullerton

■ Breast-feeding helps get your figure back after giving birth.

Jerry Hall

■ Try to use natural products and organic food whenever and wherever you can.

Jerry Hall

■ Never forget just how flattering shoulder pads can be.

Joanna Lumley

■ Drink *lots* of water.

Ali McGraw

■ Don't *ever* take your health for granted and don't underestimate the effect of the menopause.

Shirley Maclaine

■ Concentrate on your health rather than your figure and an improved appearance will follow.

Shirley Maclaine

■ Hard-boiled eggs are unfattening, full of nutrition and make a great snack (particularly the whites).

Ivana Trump

■ Rosehip tea is an excellent diuretic.

Barbara Taylor Bradford

EXERCISE

■ The best cure for water retention is exercising and perspiring.

Jacqueline Bisset

■ You can stretch and tone your body as you work in the garden or about the house.

Jacqueline Bisset

■ If you exercise at home, there's less reason not to do it.

Betsy Bloomingdale

■ Find the form of exercise that helps you face stress as well as keeping you fit. Swimming can be hugely calming.

Shakira Caine

■ Start exercising your crucial areas *earlier* rather than later. The more you do before 60 the more you can achieve at 60.

Diahann Carroll

■ Use it or lose it. Walking is one of the best forms of exercise, so get a dog! When doing any exercise the value can be increased by adding light weights to your wrists and legs.

Arlene Dahl

■ Yoga works wonders on your muscle tone, helps you to relax and improves your concentration.

Morgan Fairchild

■ A minimum of fifty sit-ups three times a week will give you a well-toned stomach, and one that you'll be able to reclaim quickly, even after childbirth.

Jerry Hall

■ Always walk up stairs rather than use the lift.

Joan Rivers

■ Be aware of your body. You can constantly exercise it, even when you're behind your desk, driving, or watching TV.

Joan Rivers

■ The mature woman's danger area – the upper arms – can be improved with a few simple daily exercises. Stand with your arms straight out, knees a little bent, back straight. Take your arms behind your back, keeping them high and straight, turn your palms upwards and then tense. Do this one hundred times.

Alana Stewart

■ For a tight butt, do leg lifts while brushing your teeth. Do fifteen on each side, stop, rotate each foot and then repeat.

Alana Stewart

■ Activity gives you more energy, which keeps you young.

Barbara Taylor Bradford

■ Kick boxing or power kicking is not only good exercise but a great de-stresser, too.

Ivana Trump

■ Just 20 minutes of simple exercises every day can make a difference. Try sitting straight in your chair, lifting your feet an inch off the ground and holding them there for as long as you can. It's excellent for the stomach muscles.

Betsy Bloomingdale

■ Keep your life full of variety; see different things and different people.

Betsy Bloomingdale

■ Never feel guilty about taking time out for yourself.

Shakira Caine

■ Be compassionate to others, but also to yourself.

Louise Fennell

■ The key to looking good is inner happiness, calm and confidence.

Fiona Fullerton

■ Moderation in all things is the key.

Joanna Lumley

LIFESTYLE

■ Getting rid of guilt is the most valuable thing a woman can do for herself.

Shirley Bassey

■ Mean thoughts make mean faces.

Jacqueline Bisset

■ Everybody, rich or poor, can be a great hostess. All it takes is imagination.

Betsy Bloomingdale

■ Entertaining is far from frivolous, think of the marriages born and friendships made at a party.

Betsy Bloomingdale

■ If you don't feel up to it, don't go to that party; only really close friends can help you out of a negative mood.

Betsy Bloomingdale

■ Deal with stress by breaking anxieties down into small manageable areas. Always give yourself rewards, like a nice cup of coffee, during a stressful day.

Joanna Lumley

■ Cat napping is invaluable. Twenty minutes spent lying down and sleeping, or just relaxing, can change the way you feel.

Joanna Lumley

■ Body obsessiveness is ultimately a turn-off. Real sexuality is about much more than the body.

Ali McGraw

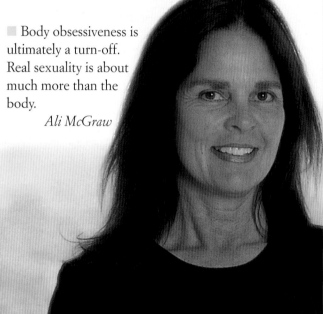

■ Work out your priorities and the people you *really* want to be with. Health is the number one importance, family the second and friends the third.

Ali McGraw

■ Listen to your soul. In life, everything happens for a purpose.

Shirley Maclaine

■ Find a place to go, or create an environment that's peaceful and restful, so there is always some place for you to relax.

Shirley Maclaine

■ 'If you do not get it from yourself, where will you go for it?'

Stefanie Powers,
from *The Zen Book of Wisdom.*

■ Eat, drink and be merry, but always in moderation.

Michelle Philips

■ Think positive. What you are feeling *inside* shows on the outside.

Alana Stewart

■ When you have your routine organised, self-maintenance really needn't take that long.

Ivana Trump

■ *Think* sexy and confident. It all starts in the head.

Ivana Trump

■ Avoid people who are a pain in the ass!

Audrey Wilder

■ If you're travelling, minimise your wardrobe; black and white trousers, drip dry shirts, co-ordinating jackets, and *no* coloured accessories.

Audrey Wilder

MY OWN 50 BEST-KEPT SECRETS

1 AFTER 40 you get the face you deserve.

2 MOISTURISE your skin every day, religiously.

3 PROTECT your face with make-up. I can vouch for the complexions of my friends over 40 – those who have always used foundation have *much* better skin than those who don't.

4 *DON'T* buy into the negativity that other people lay on you – there will *always* be knockers and pessimists trying to undermine you – don't let them sway you at all.

5 THE most flattering cosmetic is lipstick.

6 DON'T go in for trends. Slip dresses and grungy cardies only look good on stick thin adolescents. If you're over size 12 forget it.

7 LAUGHTER is one of the most beneficial mood enhancers, beautifiers and stress-busters. So laugh a lot.

8 IF you have to lose a few pounds to get into a dress for a special occasion try a two or three day fruit and vegetable dextox diet – making sure you drink plenty of water.

9 HOWEVER, crash diets may work for a few days or a few weeks but in the long run they're a no-no.

10 ONE of the best exercises for losing weight is the push-yourself-away-from-the-dining-table-before-you-eat-too-much exercise. It works.

11 SNACKS are the worst thing for weight gain – try just eating three meals a day and cut out biscuits, crisps and snacks. Weight will drop off.

12 EAT junk become junk.

13 REGULAR exercise maintains joint and muscle tone. *So use it or lose it*!

14 TOO much sleep is as bad as too little – between six and eight and a half hours is plenty.

15 DON'T *ever* soap your face and always use the mildest one possible for the body.

16 ALWAYS use bath oil.

17 YOUR age is your own business and no one else's. Oscar Wilde said, 'Never trust a woman who will tell you her age – she'll tell you anything!'

18 BRUSH your gums just as regularly as you brush your teeth. Gum disease is endemic after middle age.

19 CHANGE your shampoo and conditioner brand often. Hair flourishes better with different treaments.

20 TRY to use a face mask once a week. You can create your own using natural ingredients; egg whites and strawberries for oily skin, egg yolks or honey for dry skin, yoghurt to cleanse and avocado to counteract sun damage.

21 A LITTLE of what you fancy does you good. Don't deny yourself the glass of wine or the chocolate cake. What is life without pleasure?

22 TOMATOES, broccoli and dark green leafy vegetables are all cancer inhibitors. Also beneficial are carrots and yellow coloured vegetables.

23 ALL fruits are nutritious but papaya, mango and pineapple are particularly beneficial as they aid good digestion. Citrus fruits help protect against stomach cancer.

24 WHENEVER possible eat organic or home grown fruit and vegetables. Non-organic soft fruits, for instance, are dosed with around fifteen chemicals before reaching the shops.

25 KNOW your own type by the time you're 40 – if you've always had *ingénue* looks you won't turn into a vamp overnight. Change and experimentation is great in your teens but by the mid-30s you should know who you are and what you look like.

26 DON'T get sucked into buying an unflattering dress or suit by an eager sales assistant. They're paid commission by the stores and don't care how bad you look.

27 SHOP for clothes by yourself or with a friend whose opinion you *really* trust.

28 YOU can't stop getting older but you *can* stop getting old.

29 ACCEPT your age and the wisdom it brings.

30 CERTAIN senility problems have been known to be reversed with proper nutrition and exercise. Certain vitamin and mineral deficiencies can, over time, cause problems associated with ageing, such as anxiety and the inability to learn anything new.

31 STUDIES in the US have proven that older women who start exercising for the first time look younger, have better skin and reduced wrinkles after only one year.

32 COCO Chanel said, 'Luxury is not the opposite of poverty, it's the opposite of vulgarity.'

33 EAT lots of 'live' yoghurt. Many people from the Caucasus Mountains live to be over 100 and they believe that yoghurt which they consume regularly is one of the reasons.

34 ALWAYS eat yoghurt when taking a course of antibiotics as it restores the good bacteria which antibiotics destroy.

35 LECITHIN granules in your breakfast cereal will emulsify bad fats (cholesterol).

36 DON'T frown. Frowning causes lines even on 20-year-olds.

37 TO prevent wrinkles under eyes *always* wear sun-glasses at the slightest brightness and moisturise with eye cream or gel.

38 THE best eye cream for bags and lines is Clarins Contour des Yeux.

39 ALWAYS apply make-up to your neck too, blending it gradually so there's no tide mark. (I've been caught out *not* doing this and it looks *horrible*!)

40 GARLIC is a miracle food with an amazing amount of healthful powers. It combats a bacterium in the stomach which causes ulcers, activates enzymes which protect against cancer and decreases cholesterol and blood clot formation so helping to protect against heart disease. It's also an ancient remedy; Roman gladiators used it to keep their strength up. There's an old saying, 'Eat onions in March and garlic in May and the rest of the year your doctor can play!'

41 POSTURE can dramatically change the way you look, so sit up straight and suck in that stomach.

42 EXCESSIVE consumption of red meat increases the risk of cancer. Yes, we are carnivores but meat once or twice a week is *plenty*.

43 DON'T have too much protein. Over-eating meat, for instance, can create a residue of toxins which contributes to degenerative illnesses from gum disease to heart disease.

44 THE Hunza tribe from the Himalayas are known for their longevity. Their secret is mineral-rich water and a diet low in calories and *extremely* low in animal protein.

45 IT'S never too late to give up smoking; new research suggests that the bad effects of smoking may not be cumulative, so you could stop now and suffer no long-lasting effects.

46 NOT only does smoking cause cancer but it makes the skin on your face dramatically thinner and therefore hastens the ageing process.

47 THE sun is dangerous and ageing, so fake the sun-kissed look.

48 MARK Twain said, 'Courage is the *mastery* of fear – *not* the absence of fear.'

49 ALWAYS keep interested and enthusiastic about things. People who are bored are boring.

50 YOUR face is the mirror of your inner health – emotional, mental and spiritual.

OTHER BOOKS

The Joan Collins Beauty Book, Macmillan 1980
Katy: A Fight for Life, Gollancz 1982
Past Imperfect, Hodder 1985
Prime Time, Century 1988
Love and Desire and Hate, Arrow 1991
My Secrets, Boxtree 1994
Too Damn Famous, Orion 1995
Second Act, Boxtree 1996

PICTURE CREDITS

Cover photographs: ©Eddie Sanderson ©Richard Young

©All Action: 2, 58, 86, 93, 190
Courtesy of Anders Breinholm: 3, 115
©Jim Britt: 118, 196
Courtesy of Shakira Caine: 31
From the private collection of Joan Collins: 5, 11, 62, 67, 112, 130, 135, 143, 171, 183, 186
Courtesy of Arlene Dahl: 49
©Steve Wood/Express Picture Desk: 5, 165
Courtesy of Morgan Fairchild: 65
Courtesy of Louise Fennell: 69, 192
Courtesy of Fiona Fullerton: 81
©Ronald Grant: 17, 48, 100
Courtesy of *Hello!* Magazine: 1, 43
Courtesy of Paul Keylock: 36, 37, 53, 104, 190
©Kobal: 80, 89, 102, 116, 129, 167
©London Features: 164, 168
Courtesy of Barbara Taylor Bradford ©Lord Lichfield: 4, 150, 194
©Fiona Hanson/PA News: 13
©Michael Ochs/Redferns: 121
©David Redfern/Redferns: 1, 10, 15
©Nils Jorgensen/Rex Features: 75
Courtesy of Joan Rivers: 4, 137
©Eddie Sanderson: 1, 2, 3, 4, 5, 9, 19, 22, 24, 26, 27, 32, 35, 39, 46, 51, 54, 60, 70, 76, 79, 83, 93, 94, 95, 99, 103, 108, 109, 119, 122, 124, 126, 141, 144, 149, 157, 163, 171, 172, 174, 177, 191, 193, 194, 195, 196, 198, 203
©Scope Features: 154
Courtesy of Alana Stewart: 140, 192
©John Swannell: 6, 197, 200-1, 204-5, 208
©Julio Donoso/Sygma: 160
©Christophe Makos/Jeff Widener/Sygma: 156
©D. Rose/Sygma: 134, 138, 191
©Jeff Widener/Sygma: 159
©1982 Time Inc: 131
©Richard Young: 3, 5, 87, 91, 97, 171, 180, 193, 196

DEDICATION
For Judy Bryer and to friendship – the strongest bond of all

ACKNOWLEDGEMENTS
Grateful thanks to Hannah Macdonald for her hands-on down-to-earth
editing, and to Eddie Sanderson for his patience, good humour and
dedication in taking all the photographs

First published in Great Britain in 1999
By André Deutsch Limited
76 Dean Street W1V 5HA
www.vci.co.uk

02/04

A catalogue record for this book is available from the British Library.

ISBN 0 233 99494 7

Cover and page design © Roger Hammond
Cover photographs (except Jerry Hall & Joan Collins) © Eddie Sanderson
Cover photograph of Jerry Hall & Joan Collins © Richard Young

Printed in the UK by Butler & Tanner, Frome, Somerset and London

1 3 5 7 9 10 8 6 4 2